Contents

The material for years 3, 4 and 5 of SMP 11–16

The yellow, blue, red and green series together make up the second part of the SMP 11–16 course, for pupils in the third to fifth years of secondary school (ages 13+ to 16+).

(The booklet scheme which forms the first part of the course is fully described in the *Teacher's guides* for levels 1, 2, 3 and 4, and the *Practical guide.*)

The Y series is for the most able group of pupils (roughly speaking, the top 20% to 25% or so, although the proportion is likely to vary from school to school). The B and R series are for the 'middle' group (the next 35% to 40% or so) and the G series for lower ability pupils (apart from those with special learning difficulties).

Classroom organisation and teaching style

It is assumed that pupils will be grouped in sets according to ability in the third, fourth and fifth years.

Although there is rather more exposition and explanation in the books than is found in many other textbooks, the books are not intended to be 'self-instructional'. (This is particularly true of the chapters on algebra.) Many important points arise in the course of doing the problems in the books, and these points will need to be brought out by the teacher in discussion with the class or with smaller groups, as appropriate. Teachers may find it possible from time to time to give particular chapters or sections of chapters to the class to work through on their own, which is no bad thing since the ability to pick up information from the printed page and to follow written explanations is an important one. Where this is done it will be necessary for the teacher carefully to 'go over' what has been done. Amongst pupils working from the Y series there may be some very able ones who are quite capable of forging ahead with understanding, working from the book alone, and who should not be 'kept back'. However it is not intended that working individually through the book should be the normal method of teaching for any class, whichever series it is using. (Exceptions to this are *Books YE1* and *YE2*, and the transition books *BT* and *YT*, which are written specifically for individual use.)

There are no 'chapter summaries'. The writers feel it is more valuable for classes to make their own summary notes. The ideal ultimately is for each pupil to make his or her own notes, but initially it may be better for the teacher to lead, after each chapter, a discussion of the main ideas before any notes are made.

Introduction to Book Y5

Mental and written arithmetic and the use of calculators

It is assumed throughout that unless there is an instruction to the contrary calculators will be used for all but the simplest calculations which can be done mentally.

We strongly recommend that teachers encourage mental calculation, and from time to time give short sets of questions to be answered mentally. We also suggest having occasional practice sessions on written arithmetic, but that the scope of these should not extend beyond addition, subtraction, multiplication by 2, 3, . . . , 9 and division by 2, 3, . . . , 9 of whole numbers and money.

Starred questions

Occasional questions are starred to indicate that they are of greater difficulty, and can be left out by slower pupils using the book.

Book YE2

This 'extension' book is designed to stretch the most able pupils. It can be used alongside *Book Y5*.

Equipment needed for Book Y5

Certain standard items of equipment are needed frequently and no special attention is drawn to them in the books. These include rulers, angle measurers (recommended rather than protractors for angle measurement; see below), compasses, scissors and 2 mm graph paper.

In other cases, equipment needed (such as tracing paper) is referred to in the book. Worksheets are needed occasionally. Masters for these are available separately (see below). One worksheet is needed for *Book Y5*, numbered Y5–1.

Pupils working from the Y series are assumed to have the use of a scientific calculator from *Book Y2* onwards.

Ordering equipment

The following items required for *Book Y5* are published by Cambridge University Press. You should order them through your usual school book supplier.

Worksheet masters for *Books B5, R3, Y5* and *YE2* ISBN 0 521 33180 3
Worksheet masters for the Y series ISBN 0 521 33626 0
Angle measurers (pack of 5) ISBN 0 521 25435 3

When ordering, remember to state the ISBN, the series title (SMP 11–16), the name of the item, the publisher and the number of **packs** you want. (So, for example, if you want 35 angle measurers, write your order as '7 packs of 5'.)

Notes and answers for Book Y5

1 Surfaces

Besides being of interest in its own right, the work in this chapter provides opportunities to apply techniques introduced earlier in the course, such as Pythagoras' rule and trigonometry. Section D on the sphere is a preparation for chapter 6.

A Developable surfaces: the cylinder

Unless stated otherwise, answers are given to 1 d.p.

A1 251 mm (to nearest mm)

A2 19·1 mm

A3 (a) 15·7 cm (b) Pupil's model
(c) 18·6 cm

A4 34.6 cm

A5 (a) 9·4 cm (b) 23·0°

A6 20·9°

A7 36·3 cm

A8 (a) 63·3 cm (b) 7·3°

A9

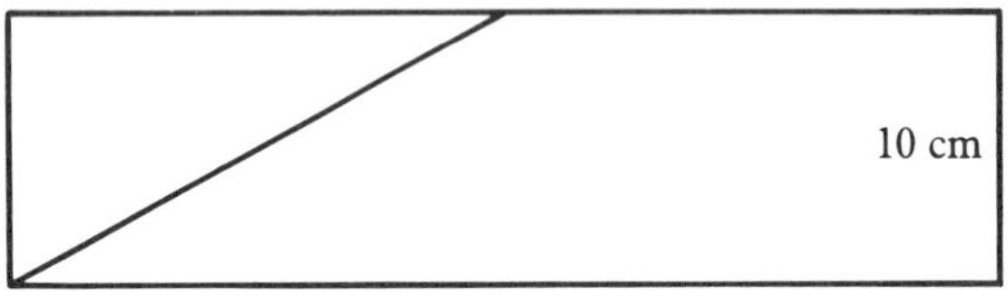

Length of helix 21·3 cm
Angle of helix 27·9°

A10 (a) Two helices (b) Four times

***A11** 27·0 cm

B Shortest paths

B1 174·9 cm

B2 67·1 cm
There are six shortest paths.

B3 (a)

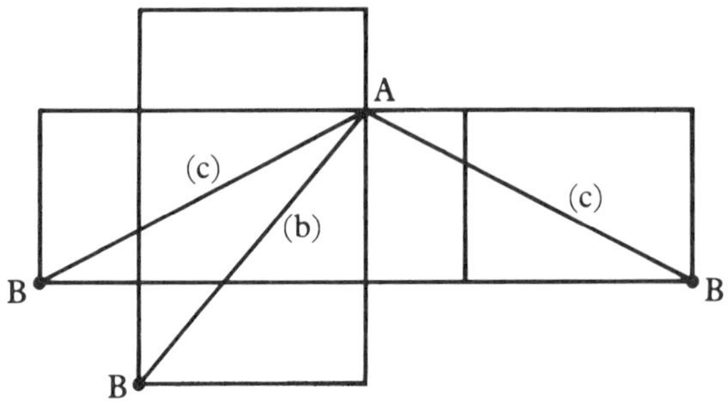

(b) 10·0 cm (c) 10·3 cm
(d) The shortest distance of 10 cm is over the 6 cm edge.

B4 48·2 cm

B5 3·7 cm

***B6** 55·9 cm

C Developable surfaces: the cone

C1 (a) 25·1 cm (b) 18·8 cm (both to 1 d.p.)
(c) 3 cm

C2 2·5 cm

C3 (a) $\frac{3}{8}$ (b) 1·2 cm

C4 (a) 288° (b) 200° (c) 72°

C5 (a) 252° (b) 1·8 m (to 1 d.p.)
(Abler pupils can be asked to solve part (b) of this question by using trigonometry.)

C6 The following answers are calculated to 1 d.p. Pupils' results, obtained by scale drawing, may differ slightly.
(a) 11·6 cm (b) 8·7 cm

D Non-developable surfaces: the sphere

D1 1·40 m (to 3 s.f.)

D2 No, the path does not lie on a great circle.

D3 50·1° (to 3 s.f.)

2 Optimisation

Optimisation problems – finding the best way of doing something – are common in industry. This chapter tries to give the flavour of some kinds of optimisation problem. In practice, of course, such problems are much more complex than those described in the chapter.

A 'Bin-packing' problems

A1 5 coaches are needed.

A2 (a) 5 planks are needed.
(b) 80 cm of wood is wasted.

A3 (a) 6 journeys are needed.
(b) The last journey will be load F on its own. One possible way is:
H (1·8); A + I (1·7 + 0·3);
D + E (1·5 + 0·4); J + G (1·5 + 0·1);
B + C (1·2 + 0·8); F (0·7).

A4 (a) Think of the pipes as 'bins' 3 units high.
(b) 4 lengths are needed.
$1\frac{3}{4} + \frac{3}{4} + \frac{1}{2}$; $1\frac{3}{4} + \frac{3}{4} + \frac{1}{2}$;
$1\frac{1}{2} + \frac{3}{4} + \frac{3}{4}$; $1 + 1 + 1$

A5 (a) 6 breaks are needed.
One possible way is:
50 + 36 + 32; 50 + 36 + 32;
50 + 36 + 25; 50 + 35 + 35;
36 + 36 + 24 + 24; 36 + 35
(b) 49 seconds

A6

Bin 1	241, 58
Bin 2	215, 77
Bin 3	205, 92
Bin 4	205, 62, 33
Bin 5	189, 111
Bin 6	176, 122
Bin 7	175, 125
Bin 8	162, 138
Bin 9	153, 106, 29, 9
Bin 10	149, 105, 45
Bin 11	99, 62, 56, 51, 24
Bin 12	49, 43, 24, 18

A7 Since the given data has a large number of items which more than half-fill the bins, the second method gives almost the same packing as in A6. The only change is that the 29 in bin 9 swaps with the 24 in bin 11.

B Maximisation subject to a constraint

B1 (a) Camera, radio, book (b) £139

B2 (a) 2 cameras (b) £170

B3 (a)

Number of Cowntrees	Number of Radburys	Weight
3	1	460 g
2	3	470 g
1	4	410 g
0	6	420 g

(b) The greatest weight is 470 g, consisting of 2 Cowntrees and 3 Radburys bars.

B4 2 lorries and 4 vans give the maximum weight of 11·0 tonnes.

B5

Dining tables	Stools	Garden seats	Profit
3	0	0	£180
2	2	0	£190
	1	1	£170
	0	2	£150
1	3	0	£165
	2	2	£160
	1	3	£140
	0	4	£120
0	5	0	£175
	4	1	£155
	3	2	£135
	2	4	£130
	1	5	£110
	0	6	£ 90

He makes his maximum profit of £190 by making 2 dining tables and 2 stools.

B6 They should pack 2 pneumatic drills and 4 grinders, to save the maximum of £264 in export costs.

Money matters: income tax

The six sections on money matters each provide a brief introduction to a financial topic. Further work on these topics is best done using up-to-date real information from tax offices, banks, building societies, etc., preferably getting the pupils to collect the data themselves. Some topics will be closer to their own interests than others.

Although the topic of income tax is generally included in mathematics courses because of the calculations involved, calculations which will be relevant to most pupils later in their lives, there are wider political issues which may already interest some pupils, and which arguably ought to be raised and discussed as part of the general education of every future citizen. (Why, for example, has it generally been accepted by all political parties that tax rates should increase as income increases, as shown in the diagram on page 19?)

3 Algebraic fractions

Multiplication and division of simple algebraic fractions were introduced in *Book Y4*. This chapter deals with addition and subtraction, and with the solution of simple equations involving algebraic fractions.

A Sums and differences of fractions

A1 $\frac{3x}{xy} + \frac{6y}{xy} = \frac{3}{y} + \frac{6}{x}$

A2 (a) $\frac{a}{c} + \frac{a}{b}$ (b) $\frac{1}{q} - \frac{2}{p}$ (c) $\frac{p}{q} + \frac{q}{p}$

(d) $3 + \frac{1}{x}$ (e) $3 - \frac{2}{a}$

A3 (a) $\frac{y + x}{xy}$ (b) $\frac{a + 2}{2a}$ (c) $\frac{ac - b}{bc}$

(d) $\frac{vx + uy}{vy}$ (e) $\frac{t - 3s}{3t}$ (f) $\frac{2x + 1}{x}$

(g) $\frac{b + 6a}{2ab}$ (h) $\frac{3 - x}{x}$ (i) $\frac{x^2 + 4}{2x}$

(j) $\frac{u^2 - v^2}{uv}$

A4 (a) $\frac{v + u}{uv}$ (b) $f = \frac{uv}{v + u}$

A5 $\frac{4a + 2bc}{8b}$

A6 (a) $\frac{4x - y}{12}$ (b) $\frac{ay + 3b}{3xy}$ (c) $\frac{5b + 2}{ab}$

(d) $\frac{p - 3}{p^2}$

A7 (a) $\frac{3a + 10}{2a^2}$ (b) $\frac{2bx + 3y}{6ab}$ (c) $\frac{y^2 - 2}{4xy}$

(d) $\frac{ay - 3x}{3x^2y}$

A8 (a) $\frac{1}{R} = 7{\cdot}5$, and so $R = 0{\cdot}133$ (to 3 s.f.)

(b) $\frac{R_2 + R_1}{R_1R_2}$ (c) $R = \frac{R_1R_2}{R_2 + R_1}$

(d) Check: $R = \frac{0{\cdot}2 \times 0{\cdot}4}{0{\cdot}4 + 0{\cdot}2} = \frac{0{\cdot}08}{0{\cdot}6} = 0{\cdot}133$

A9 $\frac{1}{f} = \frac{1}{u} + \frac{1}{v} = \frac{1}{u} + \frac{1}{mu} = \frac{m + 1}{mu}$

$u = \frac{f(m + 1)}{m}$

A10 $\frac{5x + 3}{x(x + 1)}$

A11 (a) $\frac{2b + 2 + a}{a(b + 1)}$ (b) $\frac{4x + 3y}{x(x + y)}$

(c) $\frac{2x}{a(a + 2)}$ (d) $\frac{x^2 - x + 6}{3(x - 1)}$

(e) $\frac{5x + 4}{(x + 2)(x - 1)}$ (f) $\frac{3x + 11}{(x - 3)(x + 1)}$

***A12** (a) (i) $\frac{ab}{c}$ (ii) $\frac{a}{bc}$ (iii) $\frac{p + q}{r}$

(iv) $p + \frac{q}{r}$ (v) $\frac{1}{p + \frac{1}{q}}$

(b) (i) $\overline{xy}$ (ii) $x\,\overline{y + z}$ (iii) $x\overline{z} + y$

(iv) $a\overline{b} + c\overline{d}$ (v) $(a + b)\overline{c}$

(c) (i), (iii), (iv) and (vi) are always true.

B Equations involving algebraic fractions

B1 (a) 6 (b) 0·5 (c) $^{-}1$

B2 (a) 4 (b) $^{-}2$ (c) $^{-}3$

B3 (a) 10 (b) $^{-}1{\cdot}75$ (c) $^{-}3{\cdot}4$

C Similar triangles

C1 5·4 (to 1 d.p.)

C2 5·8 (to 1 d.p.)

C3 5·14 (to 3 s.f.)

C4 5

C5 (a) Triangle EBC
(b) DA and EB are corresponding sides. So also are AC and BC.
(c) $\frac{h}{q} = \frac{x}{x+y}$
(d) $h\left(\frac{1}{p} + \frac{1}{q}\right) = \frac{h}{p} + \frac{h}{q}$
$= \frac{y}{x+y} + \frac{x}{x+y}$
$= \frac{x+y}{x+y} = 1$
(e) 2·22 (to 3 s.f.)

C6 (a) $\frac{4}{b}$ (b) $\frac{a}{5} = \frac{4}{b}$ so $ab = 20$

C7 $5x + 7y = 35$

C8 (a) ABCF is a rhombus. CF = 1
(b) EF = EC − FC = $d - 1$
(c) Triangle AFC
(d) $\frac{d}{1} = \frac{1}{d-1}$
so $d(d-1) = 1$
so $d^2 - d - 1 = 0$
(e) By measurement, d is about 1·6. By decimal search, d is 1·62 (to 2 d.p.)

C9 (a) $\frac{1}{2}p$ and 1
(b) $\frac{p}{1} = \frac{1}{\frac{1}{2}p}$
so $\frac{1}{2}p^2 = 1$
so $p^2 = 2$
so $p = \sqrt{2} = 1{\cdot}41$ (to 3 s.f.)
(c) The length of an A4 sheet is 297 mm, and its width is 210 mm.
So ratio = 1·41 (to 3 s.f.)

C10 (a) $(q - 1)$ and 1
(b) $\frac{q}{1} = \frac{1}{q-1}$
so $q^2 - q - 1 = 0$
so $q = 1{\cdot}62$ (to 2 d.p.)

4 Area under a graph

The work in this chapter gives opportunities to consolidate ideas and techniques introduced earlier, such as function notation and flowcharts. Pupils going on to *Book YE2* chapter 3 (Areas, volumes, lengths) will be expected to have covered this chapter.

B The area under a graph

B1 (a) 570 (b) 430 (c) 500

B2

Area under upper step graph	2310
Area under lower step graph	1910
So approximate area under graph	2110

B3 (a)

x	0	1	2	3	4	5	6
q(x)	2	2·1	2·4	2·9	3·6	4·5	5·6

(b) 21·1 (c) 17·5 (d) 19·3
(e) It will be slightly greater. The estimate gives a value half-way between the upper and lower areas, which corresponds with straight line segments cutting across the rectangles. The curve here is always below these straight line segements. This will apply to any curve whose gradient is always increasing.

B4 The actual area is 161·25. Pupils' approximations can be compared with this value.

B5 (a) 6·5625 (b) 6·72

B6 (a) 10·5 (b) 10·64

C The trapezium rule

C1 (a) $13{\cdot}5\,cm^2$ (b) $20\,cm^2$
(c) $19{\cdot}5\,cm^2$ (d) $14{\cdot}28\,cm^2$

C2 When $a = 0$ you have a triangle and the formula still works.

C3 975

C4 The answer depends on measurement from the drawing. The area is about $196\,cm^2$.

C5 (a) 20 m, 18·5 m, 14 m, 6·5 m
(b) $460\,m^2$ (to 2 s.f.)
(c) $69\,000\,m^3$ (to 2 s.f.)

C6 (a) At $x = 1$ and $x = 5$
(b)

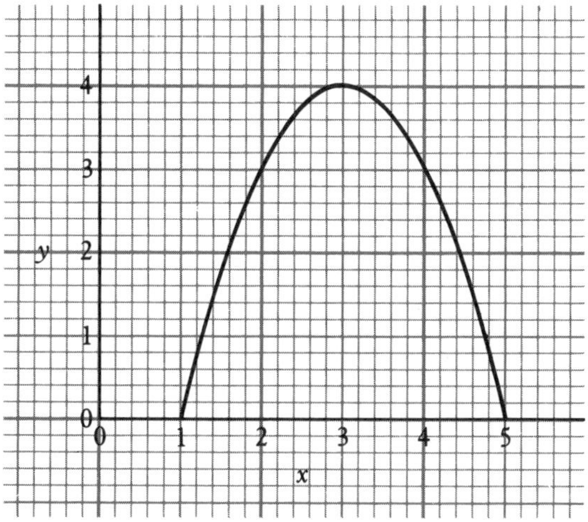

(c) 10·5
(d) The approximation is too small. All the trapeziums are below the curve.

D Area under a graph of (time, speed)

D1 (a) 32 m (b) 36 m (c) 30 m
(d) 28·5 m

D2 About 410 m

D3 200 m (to 2 s.f.)

D4 Between 1200 and 1300 litres

D5 (a)

t	r
0	10
1	5
2	2·5
3	1·25
4	0·625
5	0·3125

(b) 15 litres (to 2s.f.)

Money matters: VAT

The rate of VAT may change, as also the range of goods and services to which it applies, so up-to-date information is necessary. For a time there were different rates for different kinds of goods, and this practice could be revived. Small businesses whose yearly turnover is below a certain amount do not have to charge VAT; the threshold may be altered from time to time.

Review 1

1 Surfaces

1.1 (a) 314cm^2 (b) 33·0 cm (c) 17·7° (all to 3 s.f.)

1.2 (a)

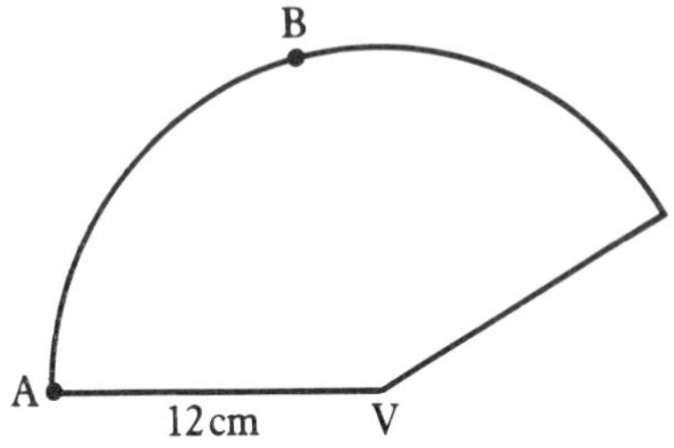

(b) 150°

(c) By calculation, 14·6 cm (to 3 s.f.)

1.3 7·91 cm (to 3 s.f.)

1.4 9·60 cm (to 3 s.f.)

2 Optimisation

2.1 (a) 5 lengths

(b) Here is one solution:
130 + 70; 75 + 65 + 60;
100 + 50 + 45; 70 + 75; 110.
Three pieces of lengths 90 cm, 55 cm and 5 cm are wasted. The 'best' solution is a matter for discussion.

2.2 A load of 1 cooker and 5 fridges has a total value of £740.

3 Algebraic fractions

3.1 (a) $\frac{3a}{4} + 3b$ (b) $\frac{a}{b} + \frac{b}{a}$

(c) $\frac{3}{y} - \frac{2}{x}$ (d) $\frac{3}{a} - 2$

3.2 (a) $\frac{2y + 3x}{xy}$ (b) $\frac{3x + 1}{x^2}$ (c) $\frac{3b - 2a}{abx}$

(d) $\frac{aq + b}{pq}$ (e) $\frac{5x + 3}{x(x + 1)}$ (f) $\frac{x - 4}{x(x - 1)}$

(g) $\frac{2a + 3b + 3}{a(b + 1)}$ (h) $\frac{2x + 16}{(x - 2)(x + 3)}$

3.3 (a) $x = 19{\cdot}1625$ (b) $x = 27{\cdot}56$
(c) $x = 0{\cdot}75$ (d) $x = 15{\cdot}5$

3.4 $x = 6{\cdot}75$

3.5 $y = 13$

4 Area under a graph

4.1 (a) 2·08 (b) 1·28 (c) 1·68 (all to 3 s.f.)

4.2 $26{\cdot}2\text{m}^2$

4.3

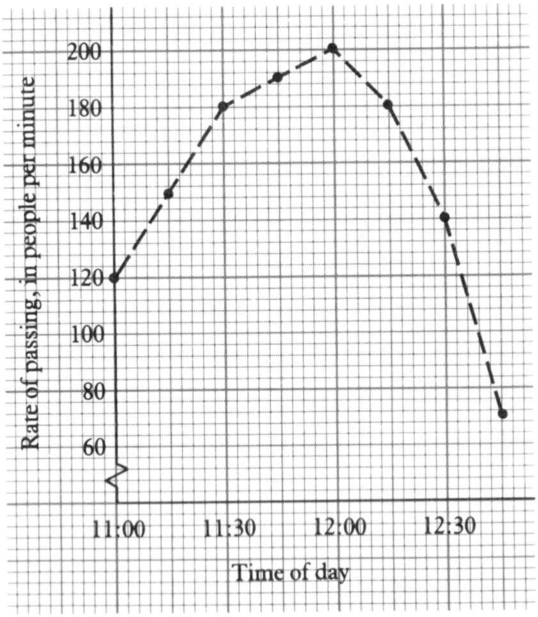

About 17 000 people

5 The sine and cosine functions (1)

In this chapter the range of definition of the sine and cosine of an angle is extended to all angles in the range 0° to 360° and the graphs of the sine and cosine functions are introduced.

A Sine and cosine: a reminder

A1 (a) a 8·2 cm, b 5·7 cm
(b) c 9·9 cm, d 6·7 cm
(c) e 9·2 cm, f 3·9 cm
(d) g 5·9 cm, h 5·4 cm
(all to nearest 0·1 cm)

B The unit circle

B1 Pupil's diagram of unit circle
(a) (0·819, 0·574) (b) (0·259, 0·966)
(all to 3 d.p.)

B2 ($^-$0·940, 0·342) (to 3 d.p.)

C The sine function

C1 (a) Pupil's graph of the sine function for $0° \leq \theta \leq 360°$
(b) Pupil's own sketch of the extended sine function graph

C2 Pupil's graph of the cosine function for $0° \leq \theta \leq 360°$

D Inverse sine

D1 (a) 140° (b) 170° (c) 65°
(d) 151° (e) 126·8° (f) 73·9°

D2 (a) 17° (b) 163° (c) Pupil's check

D3 (a) 39° or 141° (b) 49° or 131°
(c) 12° or 168°

D4 (a) (i) 143° (ii) 51° (iii) 172°
(iv) 127·4°
(b) 18° or 162° (to nearest degree)

D5 (a) $^-$34° (b) 214° or 326°

D6 231° or 309°

D7 (a) 197° or 343° (b) 27° or 153°
(c) 186° or 354° (d) 6° or 174°
(e) 244° or 296° (f) 43° or 137°

E Inverse cosine

E1 (a) 310° (b) 315° (c) 230°
(d) 245° (e) 120° (f) 20°

E2 (a) 37° (b) 323° (c) Pupil's check

E3 (a) 45° or 315° (b) 71° or 289°
(c) 66° or 294°

E4 (a) 215° (b) Pupil's check

E5 (a) 120° or 240° (b) 127° or 233°
(c) 98° or 262°

E6 (a) 39° or 141° (b) 236° or 304°
(c) 78° or 282° (d) 112° or 248°
(e) 12° or 168° (f) 71° or 289°

Money matters: insurance

Vehicle insurance and holiday insurance are likely to be of some interest to pupils. As in the case of the other financial topics, there is no adequate substitute for collecting real data. It is instructive to compare the premiums charged and the coverage offered by different companies for similar classes of insurance, for example a two-week stay in Europe.

1 People on winter sports holidays have more accidents.

2 (a) £135 (b) £126

6 The Earth

This chapter explains the method of describing the location of a point on the Earth's surface by latitude and longitude. Sections D and E look at the problem of making a flat map of the Earth's surface, and some of the different ways of tackling the problem. A full discussion of this topic requires mathematics beyond the scope of the course, but some of the main ideas are accessible and it is hoped that pupils will be encouraged to read these sections for general interest.

A Great circles

A1 About 40 000 km

A2 About 20 000 km

A3 About 10 000 km

A4 One ten-millionth

A5 About 20 000 km

B Latitude

B1 (a) North pole (b) 90°S
(c) Points on the equator

B2 6700 km (to 2 s.f.)

B3 (a) 1700 km (b) 8400 km
(both to 2 s.f.)

B4 (a) London (b) Auckland
(c) Sydney

B5 (a) $51\frac{1}{2}$°S (b) 37°N

C Longitude

C1 Pupil's explanation of why 180°E is the same as 180°W

C2 (a) 150°E (b) 120°W (c) 180°E or W

C3 156°W

C4 A 30°N 30°E, B 20°N 60°E,
C 20°N 20°W, D 50°N 10°W,
E 60°N 90°E

C5 A 30°S 150°W, B 20°S 120°W,
C 20°S 160°E, D 50°S 170°E,
E 60°S 90°W

D Map projections

D1 No, the red line does not lie on a great circle.

D2 Yes

D3 No, the area nearest the equator is larger on the globe.

D4 No, only the equator is a great circle.

D5 The north pole is the 90°N line.

D6 CP = OP cos 40°
The circumference is about 31 000 km (to 2 s.f.).

D7 (a) 35 000 km (b) 28 000 km
(c) 20 000 km (d) 10 000 km
(all to 2 s.f.).

E Further map projections

E1 No, look at the plan view at the bottom of the page.

E2 It is what you see when you look down from above the north pole.

E3 About 72°N

E4 Lines of latitude get further apart towards the equator.

Money matters: foreign exchange

As is the case of the other topics in this series, up-to-date information is needed to bring the topic to life. Although most people are directly interested in exchange rates only when they are going abroad, there remain in the background wider issues, such as what determines exchange rates and what causes them to change.

1 (a) 593F (b) 948·80F

2 £42·16 (to nearest penny)

3 £2·95, £4·55 and £6·07 (all to nearest penny)

7 Equations and graphs

This chapter takes an overall look at some 'standard' types of graph: $y = ax$, $y = ax + b$, $y = ax^2$ and $y = \frac{a}{x}$. Section D deals with fitting a linear equation to a set of data by a graph, and section E introduces the technique of transforming a relationship into a linear form for the purpose of fitting.

A The graph of $y = ax$

A1 Gradients 3, 1 and $\frac{1}{2}$

A2 (a)

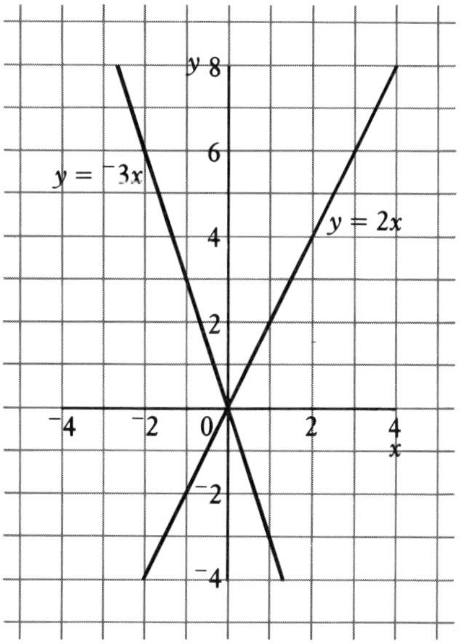

(b) (i) 2 (ii) $^{-}3$

A3 (a) A straight line through the origin with a gradient of 100
(b) A straight line through the origin with a gradient of $^{-}100$

A4 Because $a \times 0 = 0$ whatever the value of a

A5 (a) a: 0·3; b: $^{-}0{\cdot}2$
(b) a: $y = 0{\cdot}3x$; b: $y = {}^{-}0{\cdot}2x$

B The graph of $y = ax + b$

B1 Line a: (i) 0 (ii) $y = \frac{1}{3}x$
Line b: (i) 2 (ii) $y = \frac{1}{3}x + 2$
Line c: (i) 3 (ii) $y = \frac{1}{3}x + 3$
Line d: (i) $^{-}1$ (ii) $y = \frac{1}{3}x - 1$
Line e: (i) $^{-}3$ (ii) $y = \frac{1}{3}x - 3$

B2 Line a: $y = {}^{-}0{\cdot}4x$
Line b: $y = {}^{-}0{\cdot}4x + 4$
Line c: $y = {}^{-}0{\cdot}4x + 6$
Line d: $y = {}^{-}0{\cdot}4x - 2$

B3 (a) $y = \frac{1}{3}x + 2$

(b) $y = 1{\cdot}25x - 5$

(c) $y = {}^{-}0{\cdot}5x + 4$

B4 Line a: $y = {}^{-}0{\cdot}2x + 14$

Line b: $y = 0{\cdot}4x - 4$

C The graphs of $y = ax^2$ and $y = \frac{a}{x}$

C1

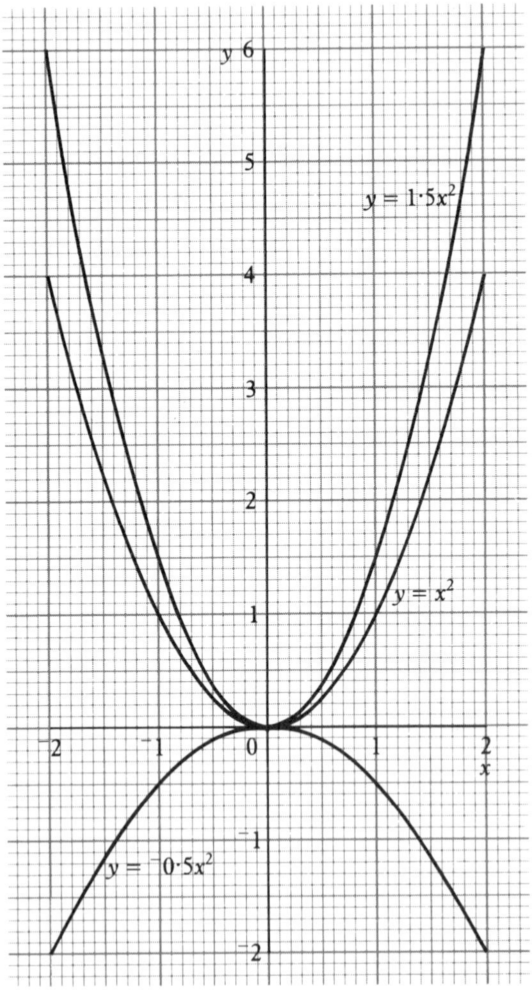

C2

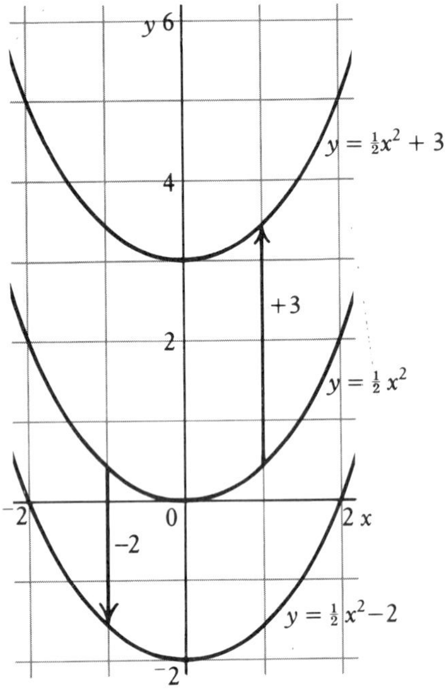

C3 (a)

x	0·5	1	1·5	2	3	4	5	6
y	6	3	2	1·5	1	0·75	0·6	0·5

(b) Division by 0 is not possible.

(c)

x	$^{-}6$	$^{-}5$	$^{-}4$	$^{-}3$	$^{-}2$	$^{-}1{\cdot}5$	$^{-}1$	$^{-}0{\cdot}5$
y	$^{-}0{\cdot}5$	$^{-}0{\cdot}6$	$^{-}0{\cdot}75$	$^{-}1$	$^{-}1{\cdot}5$	$^{-}2$	$^{-}3$	$^{-}6$

(d)

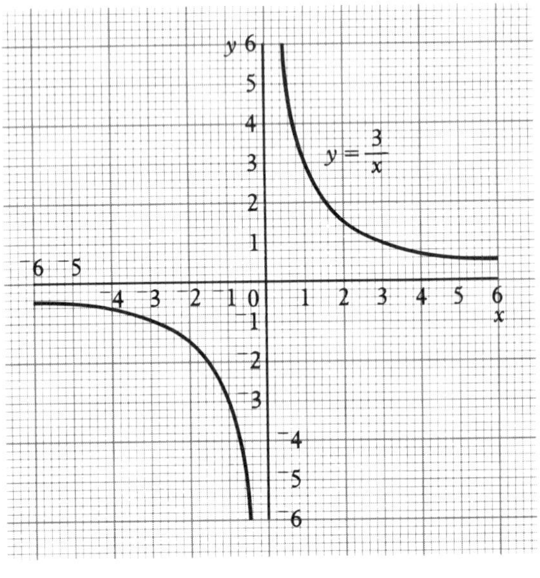

C4 (a) $y = 4 - 0{\cdot}3x^2$ (b) $y = \dfrac{2}{x}$
(c) $y = 2{\cdot}5x$ (d) $y = 4 - 0{\cdot}6x$
(e) $y = 0{\cdot}8x$ (f) $y = 0{\cdot}8x^2$
(g) $y = 1{\cdot}5x - 2$ (h) $y = 0{\cdot}3x^2 + 4$

D Fitting a linear equation

D1 (a) 0·5 (b) 55 (c) $m = 0{\cdot}5t + 55$

D2 (a)

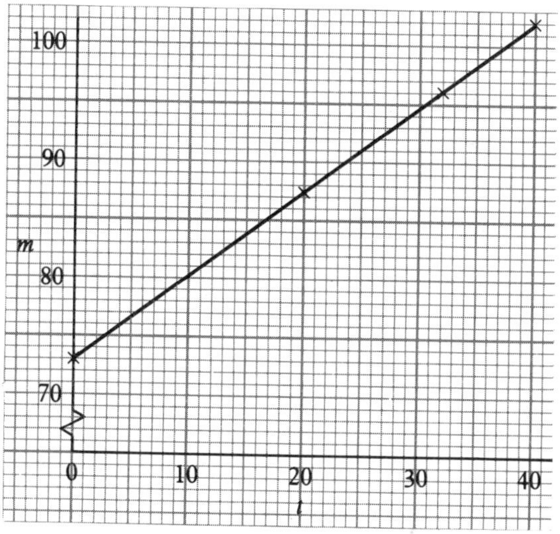

(b) About $m = 0{\cdot}73t + 73$

D3 (a)

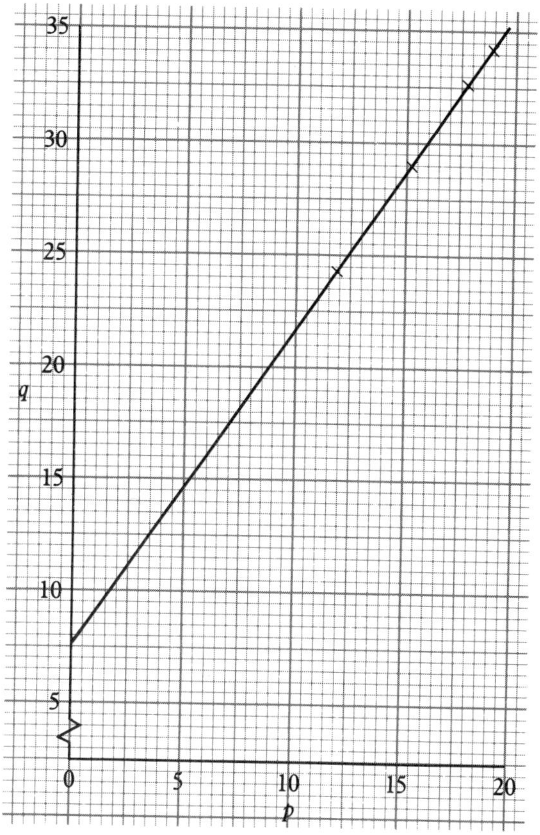

(b) About $q = 1{\cdot}4p + 7{\cdot}6$

D4

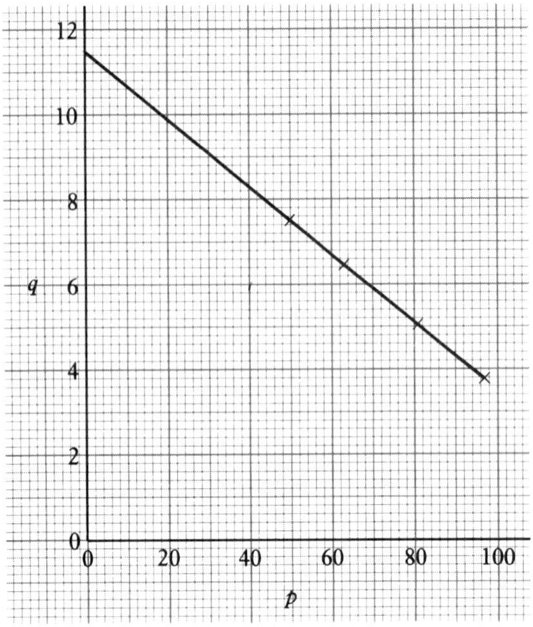

About $q = {}^{-}0{\cdot}08p + 11{\cdot}5$

E Fitting other equations

E1

$x(=p^2)$	9·0	21·16	27·04	36·0	54·76
$y(=q)$	24·5	30·6	33·5	38·0	47·4

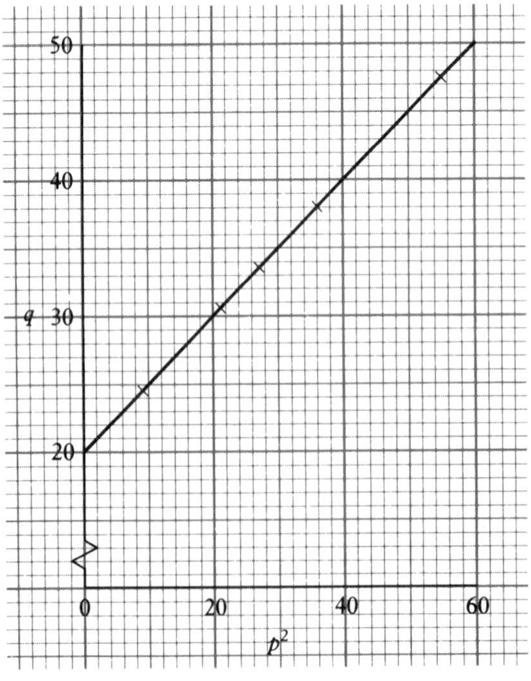

$a = 0{\cdot}5,\ b = 20$ (approx.)

E2

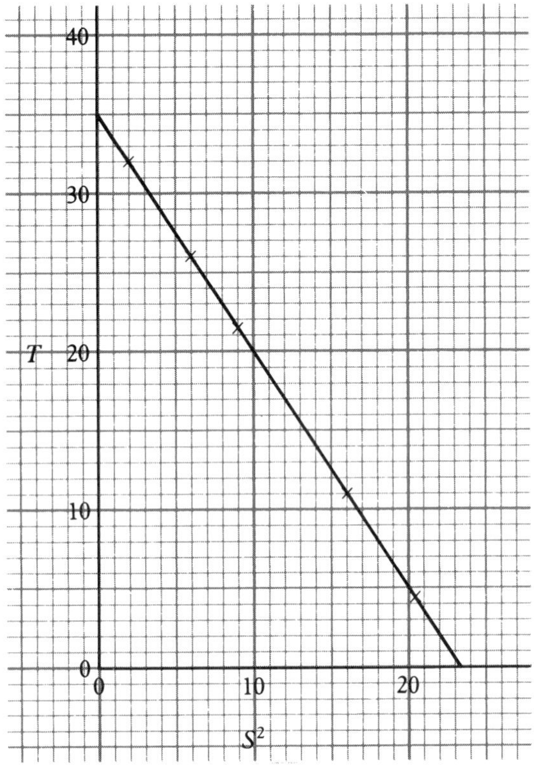

$a = {}^{-}1{\cdot}5,\ b = 35$ (approx.)

E3 (a)

$x(=\sqrt{p})$	1·18	1·82	2·68	3·26	3·97
$y(=q)$	11·5	13·0	15·2	16·6	18·4

(b)

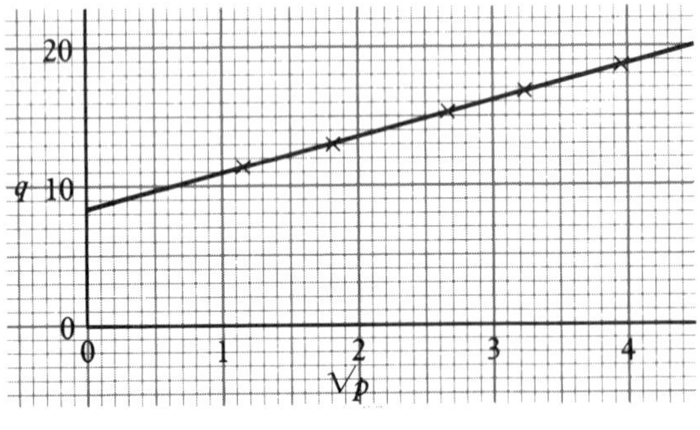

$a = 2{\cdot}5,\ b = 8{\cdot}5$ (approx.)

(c) Pupil's check

E4

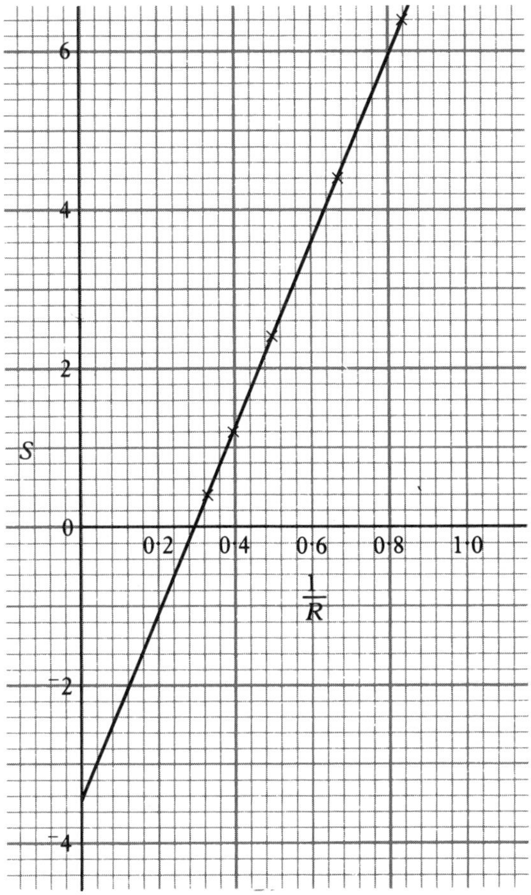

$a = 12,\ b = {}^-3{\cdot}6$ (approx.)

8 Three dimensions

This chapter represents a culmination of work in three dimensions throughout the course. In section A, views are used to explain why objects look as they do in perspective; included in this section are some problems in perspective drawing. (For those pupils who have not already used it, the level 4(e) booklet *Mathematics from pictures* provides an additional resource.) Section B is about orthographic projection, which is the name used to describe the method by which plan-and-elevation type views are produced, and shows how such a view differs from a perspective view. Section C looks briefly at other kinds of projection. In section D three-dimensional coordinates are introduced.

A Perspective

A1

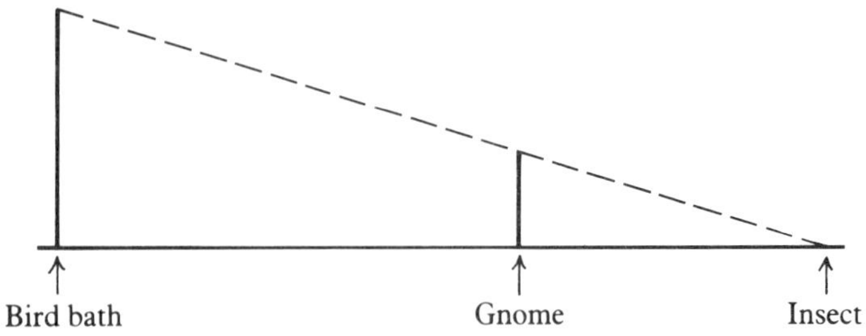

A2 (a)

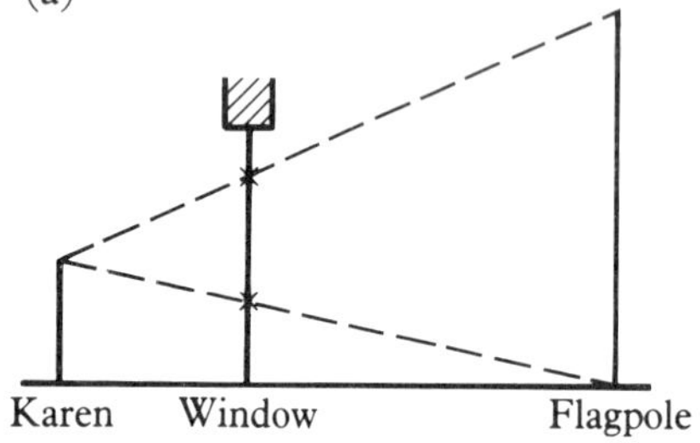

(b)

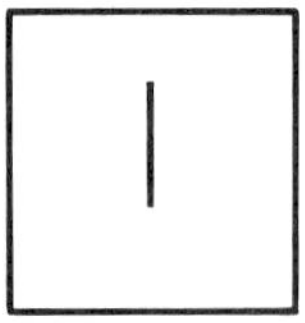

A3 (b)

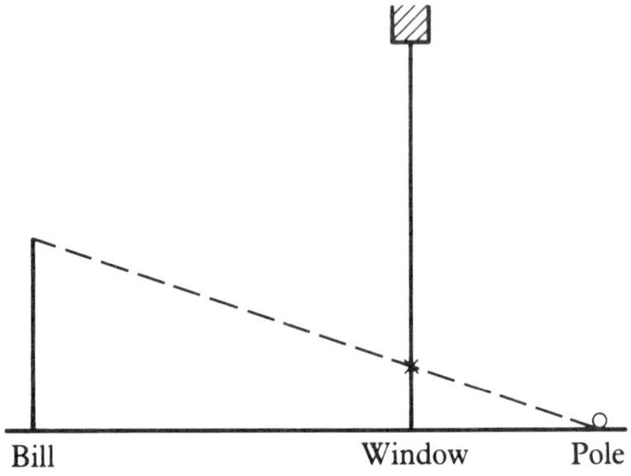

(c)

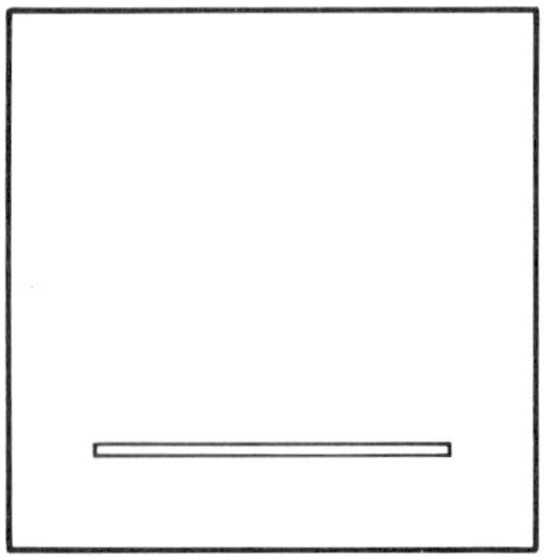

A3 (a)

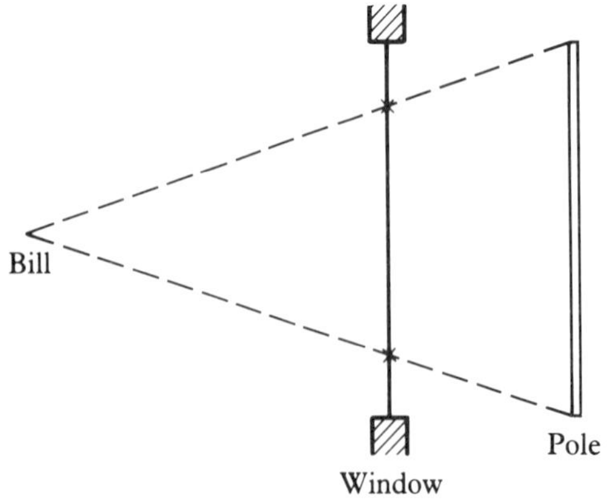

A4

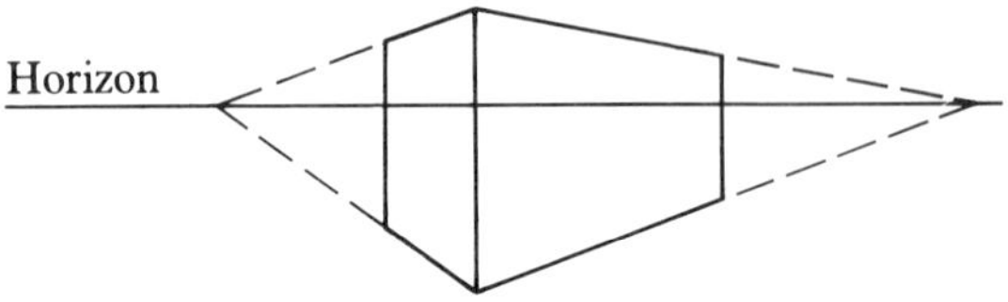

A5

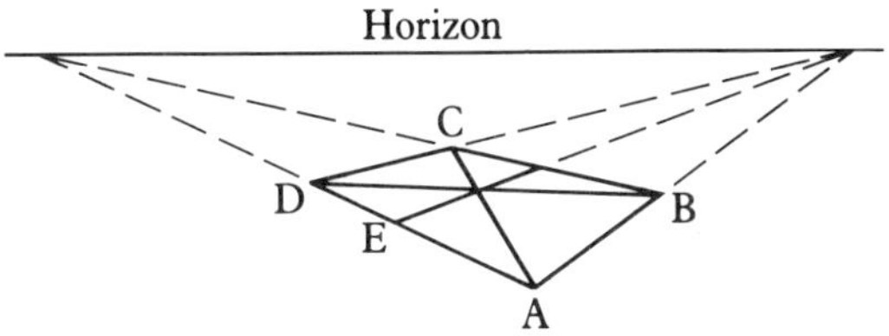

(c) AE and ED are equal in the real rectangle.

A6 (a) EE′ > DD′ > CC′ and so on

(b) The real posts A′, B′, C′, D′ and E′ are equally spaced.

(c)

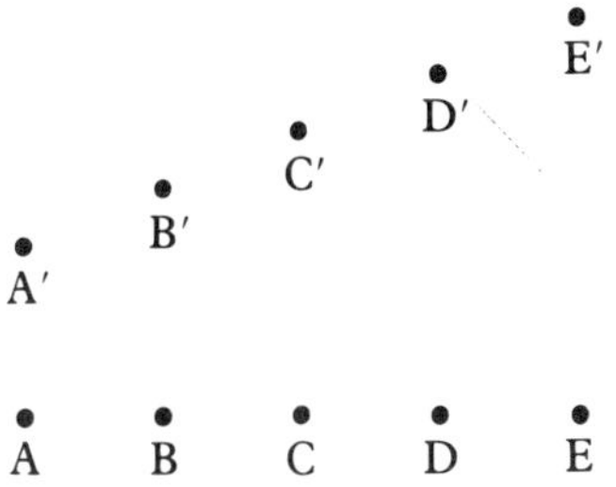

A7

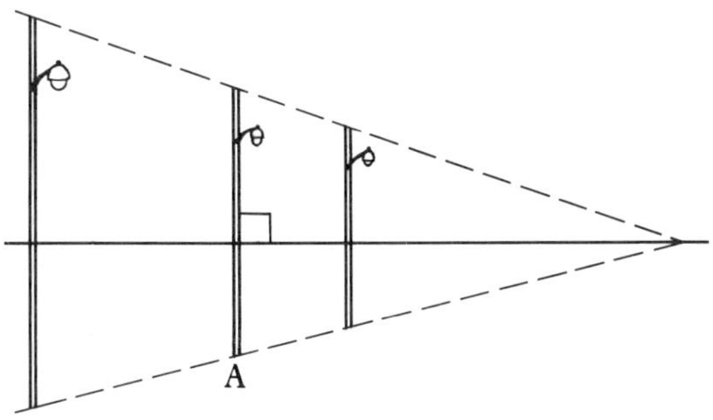

A8

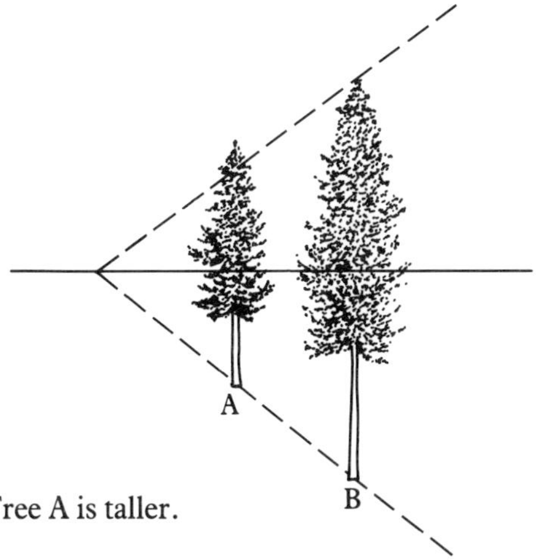

Tree A is taller.

A9

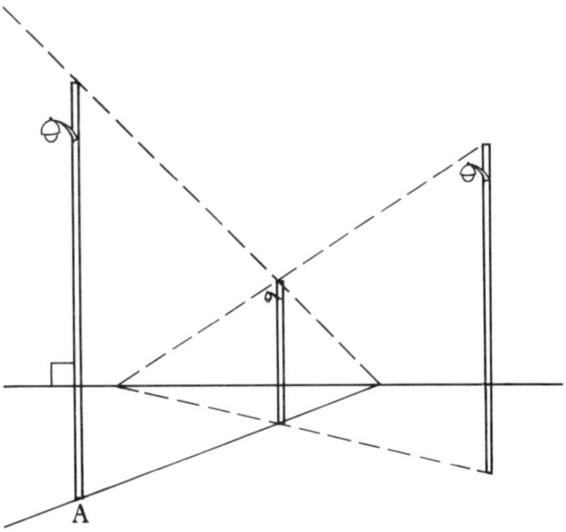

A10

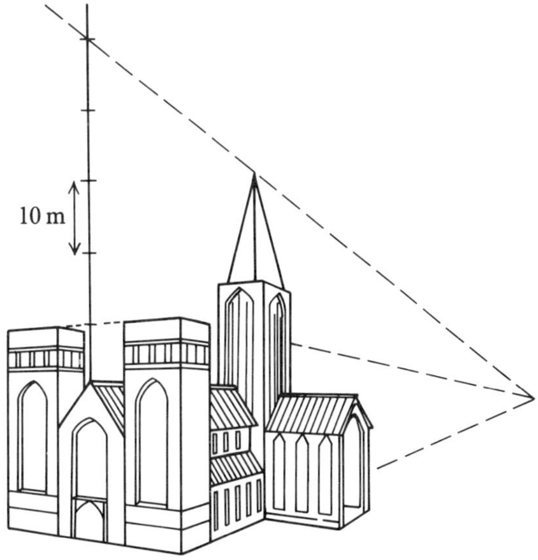

The height of the spire is about 70 m.

B Orthographic projection

B1 (a) Views B and C

(b) Find the slant height of the roof from B. Find the length of the roof from A or C. Multiply these together to find the area of one side, and double this result. The area is about 21 m^2 (to 2 s.f.), using 2·2 m as the slant height and 2·8 m as the length of the roof.

B2

(a)

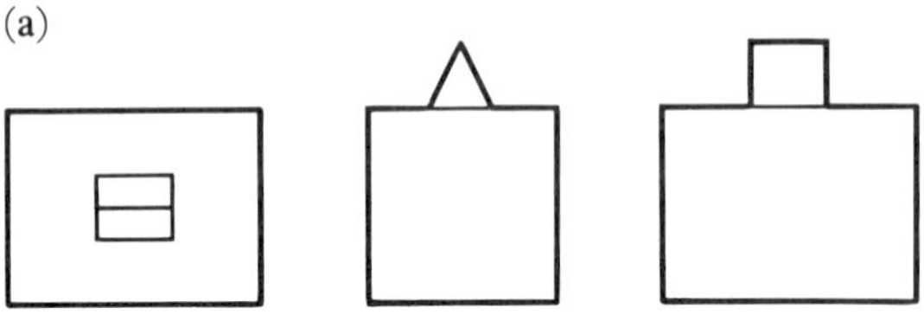

(b)

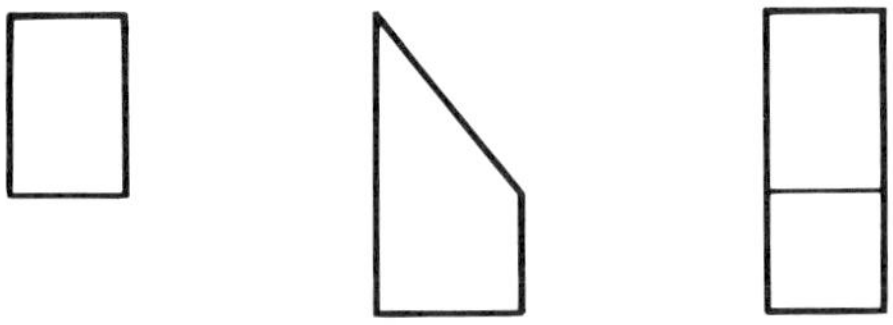

B3

(a) a 2·8 cm, b 2·7 or 2·8 cm, c 1·6 cm, d 1·6 cm

(b) 2·3 or 2·4 cm

B4

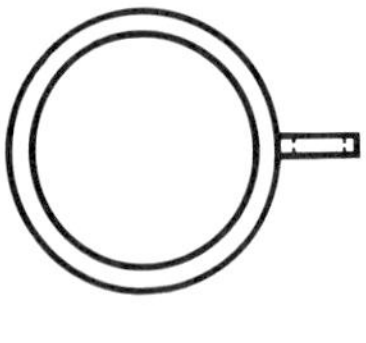

B5

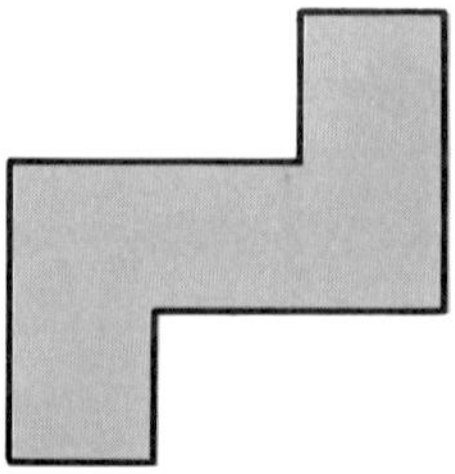

B6

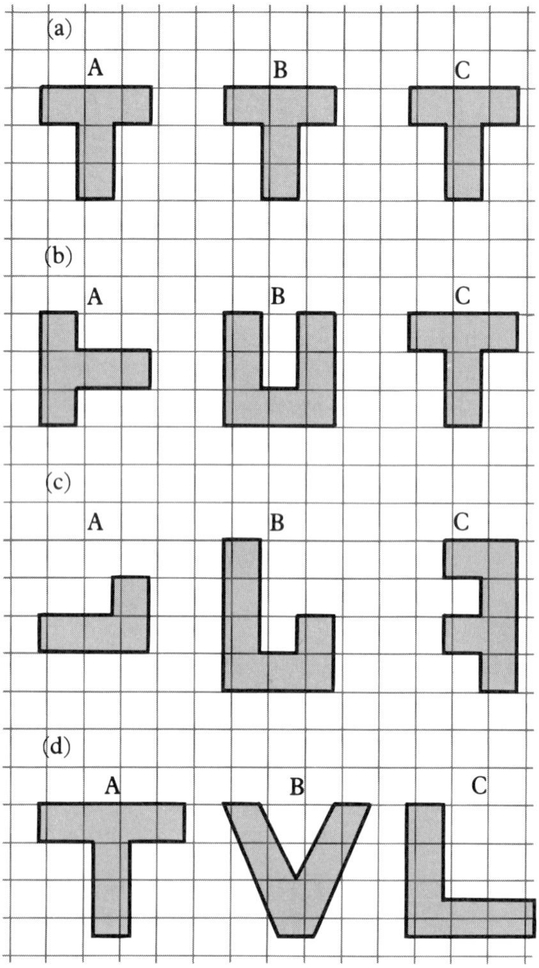

B6

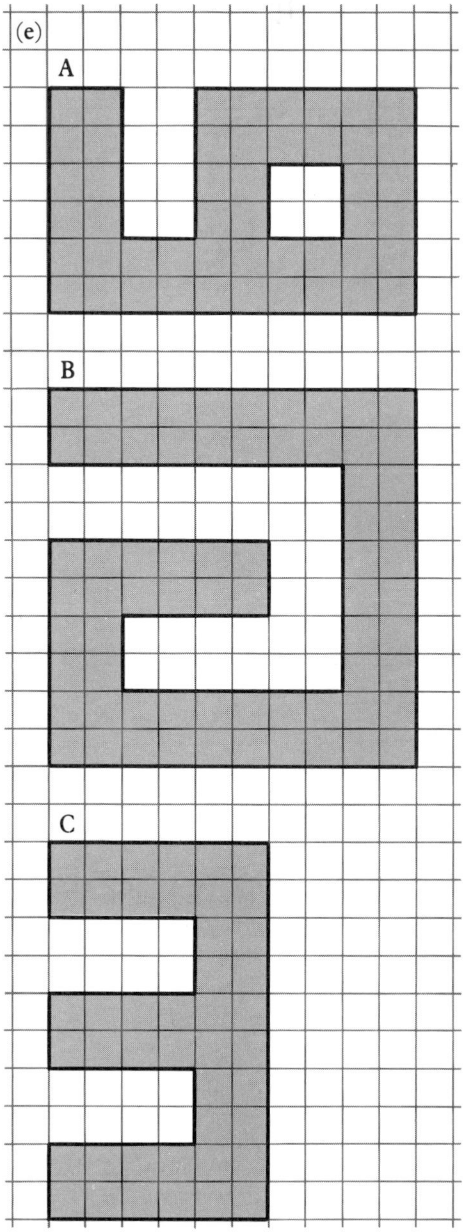

B7

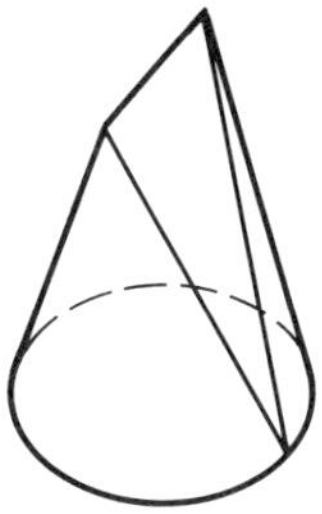

D Coordinates in three dimensions

D1 A(0, 0, 0), B(3, 0, 0), C(3, 3, 0), D(0, 3, 0), E(0, 0, 3), F(3, 0, 3), G(3, 3, 3), H(0, 3, 3)

D2 (a) (0, 1·5, 3) (b) (3, 1·5, 3) (c) (1·5, 1·5, 0)

D3 (a) (1·5, 0, 1·5) (b) (1·5, 3, 1·5) (c) (3, 1·5, 1·5)

D4 (1·5, 1·5, 1·5)

D5 A(2, 4, 6), B(2, 4, 4), C(4, 3, 4), D(4, 4, 3), E(5, 3, 3), F(6, 4, 2)

D6 PQ = 6·40, QR = 5·83, PR = 5·00 (all to 3 s.f.)

D7 (a) A(6, 0, 5), B(9, 5, 2), C(4, 7, 3)
(b) D(4·5, 5·25, 6·5)
(c) 3·16 m (d) 18·4° (both to 3 s.f.)
(e) 5·5 m

Three-dimensional puzzles

1 Some possible letters are given below. Much discussion will be needed here, and an analysis of the pupils' sketches.
(a) H, K, N, U
(b) M, V, W, X, Y
(c) I
(d) B, C, D, E, F, G, I, J, O, P, Q, R, S, T, Z
(e) K, L
(f) W
(g) A, V, X, Y
(h) B, E, G, Q, R
(i) A

2

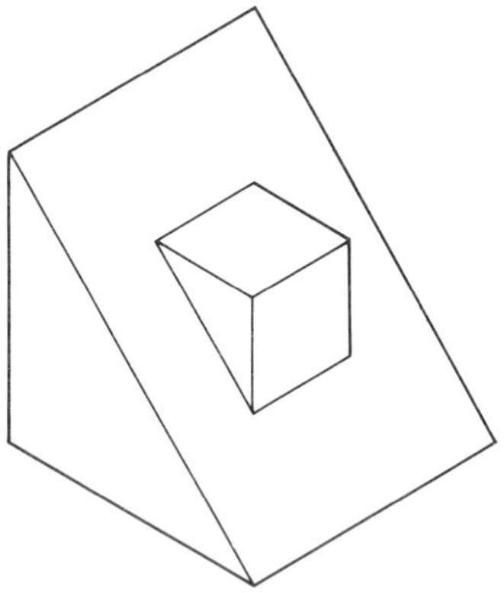

Review 2

5 The sine and cosine functions (1)

5.1 (a) About 37°, 143° (b) 143·1°

5.2

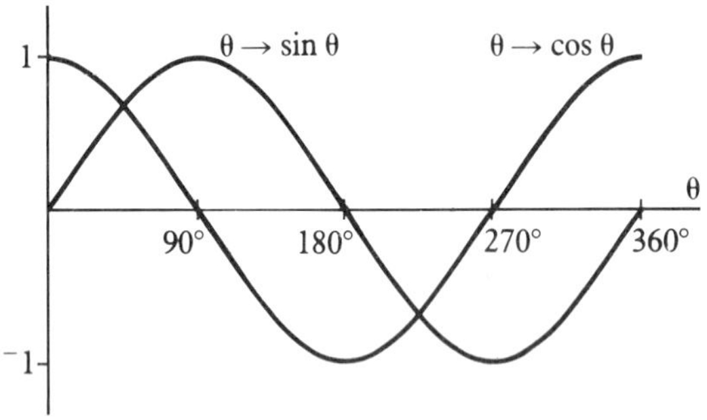

5.3 41° and 319°

5.4 14° and 166°

5.5 (a) 26° and 154° (b) 46° and 314°
(c) 200° and 340° (d) 146° and 214°
(e) 85° and 275° (f) 95° and 265°
(g) 5° and 175° (h) 185° and 355°
(all to the nearest degree)

6 The Earth

6.1 A 30°N 60°E, B 60°N 150°E, C 30°N 150°W

6.2 A 30°S 120°W, B 60°S 30°W, C 30°S 30°E

6.3 (a) 4150 miles (b) 8290 miles
(c) 12 400 miles (all to 3 s.f.)

7 Equations and graphs

7.1 (a) $\frac{2}{3}$ (b) $y=\frac{2}{3}x$
(c) $y=\frac{2}{3}x+2$ (d) $y=\frac{2}{3}x-3$

7.2 Line a: (i) 1 (ii) 3 (iii) $y=x+3$
Line b: (i) $^{-}2$ (ii) 1 (iii) $y={}^{-}2x+1$
Line c: (i) $^{-}\frac{1}{4}$ (ii) 5 (iii) $y={}^{-}\frac{1}{4}x+5$
Line d: (i) $\frac{1}{3}$ (ii) $^{-}3$ (iii) $y=\frac{1}{3}x-3$

7.3 A $y=2-2x$, B $y=x^2-2$,
C $y=\frac{^{-}2}{x}$, D $y=2x^2$,
E $y=\frac{1}{2}x-2$, F $y=2+2x$,
G $y=2-x^2$, H $y=\frac{1}{2}x^2$,
I $y=2+x^2$, J $y=\frac{2}{x}$,
K $y=2-\frac{1}{2}x$, L $y=2+\frac{1}{2}x$

7.4

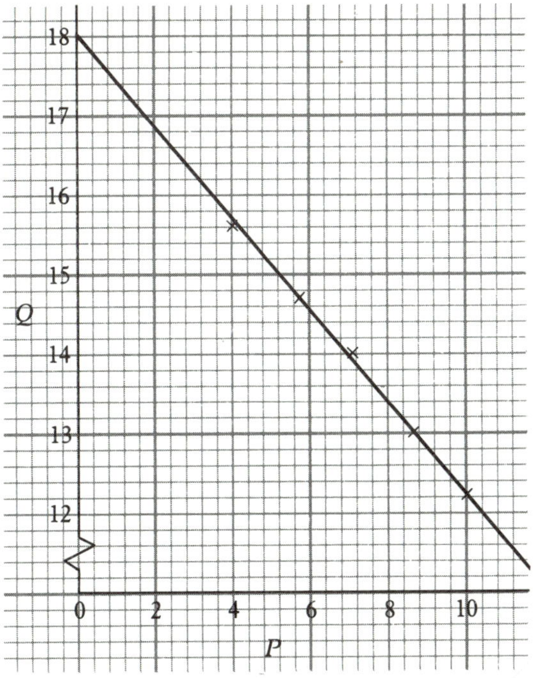

$a = {}^{-}0{\cdot}6$, $b = 18$ (approx.)

7.5

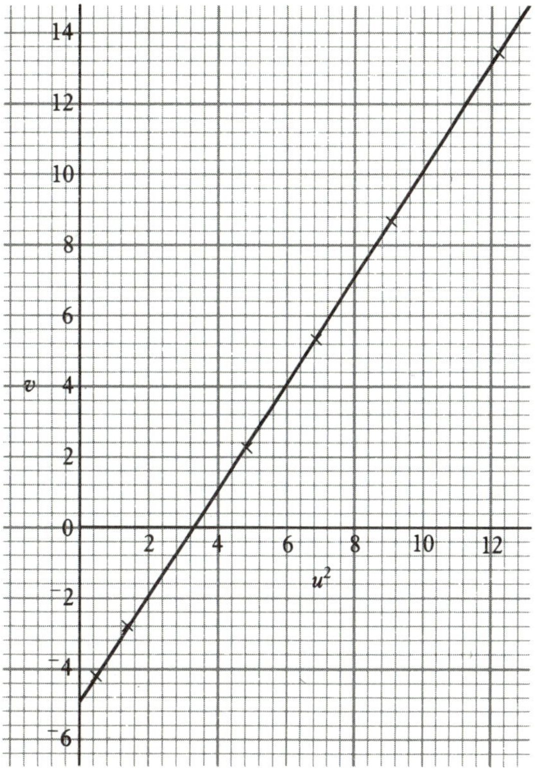

$a = {}^{-}0{\cdot}6$, $b = 18$ (approx.)

a = 1.5 b = ⁻5

8 Three dimensions

8.1 (a) $15{\cdot}5\,\text{m}^2$ (b) $25{\cdot}9\,\text{m}^2$ (to 1 d.p.)

8.2

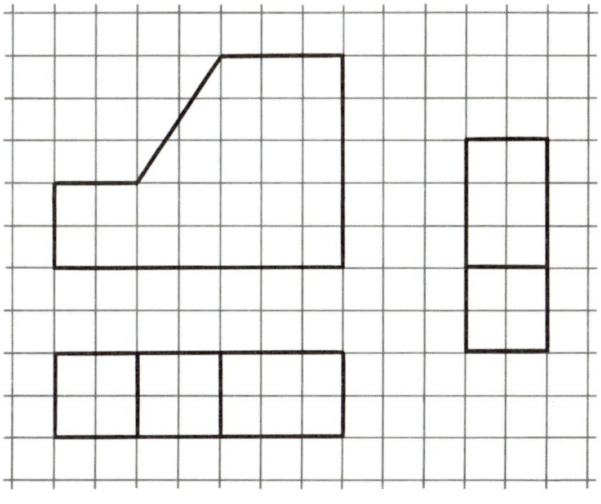

8.3 (2, 4, 0), (2, 0, 5), (0, 4, 5), (2, 4, 5)

9 Iteration

This chapter is a continuation of the work on sequences begun in *Book Y4*. After a brief revision of suffix notation and iteration formulas, the chapter introduces in an informal way the idea of a limit of a sequence and goes on to relate limits and fixed points of an iteration formula. Section D shows how fixed points can be found by solving an equation algebraically, and section E reverses this procedure to give a method for solving an equation by iteration. Section F looks at some complications which can arise.

A The limit of a sequence

A1 1, 3, 5, 7, 9, 11, 13, 15, 17, 19

A2 8, 13, 18, 23

A3 60, 90, 135, 202·5

A4 (a) 9, 19, 39, 79, 159
(b) 9, 3, 1·732, 1·316, 1·147 (to 3 d.p.)
(c) 9, 20, 42, 86, 174

A5 6, 5·2, 5·04, 5·008

A6 Sequence: 8, 7, 6·5, 6·25, ...
Limit: 6

A7 Sequence: 6, 7·5, 7·875, 7·96875, ...
Limit: 8

A8 Sequence: 2, 5·5, 5·181 8182, 5·192 9825, 5·192 5676
Limit: 5·19 (to 2 d.p.)

B Fixed points

B1 See the graph on page 108 of the pupil's text.

B2 (a) 12, 6, 4, 3·333, 3·111, 3·037 (to 3 d.p.)
(b) 3
(c) 2, 2·667, 2·889, 2·963, 2·988, 2·996 (to 3 d.p.)
Yes, this sequence does converge towards 3.
(d) 3, 3, 3, 3, 3, 3
3 is a fixed point of the iteration formula.

B3 (a) 32, 8, 3·2, 2·24, 2·048, 2·0096
(b) 2
(c) When $r_1 = 2$, $r_2 = \dfrac{2+8}{5} = 2$ ✓

B4 (a) Sequence depends on pupil's choice of s_1. The limit is 16.
(b) For $s_1 = 16$, $s_2 = \dfrac{16}{4} + 12 = 16$ ✓

B5 (a) 5, 11, 29, 83, 245, 731
This sequence does not converge.
(b) 1, $^{-}1$, $^{-}7$, $^{-}25$, $^{-}79$, $^{-}241$
This sequence does not converge.
(c) The fixed point is 2.

B6 0·5, 0·707, 0·541, 0·677, 0·568, 0·657, 0·585, 0·644, 0·597, 0·635 (to 3 d.p.)
When $s_1 = 0{\cdot}618$, $s_2 = 0{\cdot}618$ (to 3 d.p.) ✓
So 0·618 is, approximately, a fixed point.

C Iteration formulas with more than one fixed point

C1

v_1	v_2	v_3	v_4	v_5	v_6	v_7	v_8	**Behaviour**
3	0·5	1·333	0·857	1·077	0·963	1·019	0·991	Converges to 1
2	0·667	1·2	0·909	1·048	0·977	1·012	0·994	Converges to 1
1	1	1	1	1	1	1	1	Fixed point
0	2	0·667	1·2	0·909	1·048	0·977	1·012	Converges to 1
−1								Involves division by 0
−2	−2	−2	−2	−2	−2	−2	−2	Fixed point
−3	−1							Involves division by 0
−4	−0·667	6	0·286	1·556	0·783	1·122	0·943	Converges to 1

C2 It is not possible to find a sequence which converges to the fixed point, −2.

C3 The fixed points are 0 and 1.
(a) When $w_1 > 1$, the sequence diverges.
(b) When $0 < w_1 < 1$, the sequence converges to 0.
(c) When $^-1 < w_1 < 0$, the sequence converges to 1.
When $w_1 < {^-1}$, the sequence diverges.

D Fixed points and equations

D1 (a) 6, 4·666 6667, 4·222 2222, 4·074 0741, 4·024 6914, 4·008 2305
The sequence appears to converge to 4.
(b) Check: When $u_1 = 4$, $u_2 = \frac{4+8}{3} = 4$ ✓

D2 (a) 6
(b) 10, 7, 6·25, 6·0625, 6·015 625, 6·003 9063
The sequence does converge. The fixed point is 6.

D3 (a) 3 (b) 2·5 (c) 14 (d) 9
(e) −1 (f) 2

D4 When $u_1 = {^-3}$, $u_2 = \frac{6}{^-3+1} = {^-3}$ ✓

When $u_1 = 2$, $u_2 = \frac{6}{2+1} = 2$ ✓

D5 The fixed points are −5 and 3.
When $u_1 = {^-5}$, $u_2 = \frac{15}{^-5+2} = {^-5}$ ✓

When $u_1 = 3$, $u_2 = \frac{15}{3+2} = 3$ ✓

D6 The fixed points are −2 and 9.

D7 (a) −8 and 2 (b) −7 and 3 (c) 2 and 3

E Solving equations by iteration (1)

E1 (a) 2, 2·5, 2·4, 2·416 6667, 2·413 7931, 2·414 2857
The sequence converges to a limit of 2·41 (to 2 d.p.)
(b) When $u_1 = 2{\cdot}41$, $u_2 = \frac{1}{2{\cdot}41} + 2$
$= 2{\cdot}4149378$ ✓

E2 (a) $u_{n+1} = \frac{5}{u_n + 3}$
(b) 1, 1·25, 1·176 4706, 1·197 1831, 1·191 2752, 1·192 9544
The limit is 1·19 (to 2 d.p.)
(c) When $u_1 = 1{\cdot}19$, $u_2 = \frac{5}{1{\cdot}19 + 3}$
$= 1{\cdot}1933174$ ✓

E3 (a) $x = \frac{10}{x+2}$
(b) $u_{n+1} = \frac{10}{u_n + 2}$
(c) 3, 2, 2·5, 2·222222, 2·368 4211, 2·289 1566, 2·331 4607, 2·308 69
The limit is 2·3 (to 1 d.p.)
(d) Check: $2{\cdot}3 \times (2{\cdot}3 + 2) = 9{\cdot}89$ ✓

E4 (a) $x = \frac{20}{x+3}$ (b) $u_{n+1} = \frac{20}{u_n + 3}$
(c) 3, 3·333 3333, 3·157 8947, 3·247 8633, 3·201 0944
The limit is 3·2 (to 1 d.p.).
(d) Check: $3{\cdot}2(3{\cdot}2 + 3) = 19{\cdot}84$ ✓

E5 1, 1·6666667, 1·3636364, 1·4864865, 1·4341085, 1·4559819, 1·4467668, 1·4506348, 1·4490087, 1·4496919, 1·4494048
The limit is 1·45 (to 2 d.p.).
Check: $1{\cdot}45^2 + (2 \times 1{\cdot}45) - 5 = 0{\cdot}0025$ ✓

E6 (a)
$$x^2 + 5x = 10$$
Factorise. $x(x+5) = 10$
Divide both sides by $x + 5$. $x = \dfrac{10}{x+5}$

(b) $u_{n+1} = \dfrac{10}{u_n + 5}$

(c) 1, 1·666667, 1·5, 1·5384615, 1·5294118, 1·5315315, 1·5310345
The limit is 1·53 (to 2 d.p.).

(d) Check: $1{\cdot}53^2 + (5 \times 1{\cdot}53) = 9{\cdot}9909$ ✓

E7 (a)
$$x^2 - 3x - 5 = 0$$
$$x^2 - 3x = 5$$
$$x(x-3) = 5$$
$$x = \frac{5}{x-3}$$

(b) $u_{n+1} = \dfrac{5}{u_n - 3}$

(c) 5, 2·5, $^-$10, $^-$0·38461, $^-$1·4772727, $^-$1·1167513, $^-$1·2145499, $^-$1·1863663, $^-$1·1943532, $^-$1·1920789
The limit is $^-$1·19 (to 2 d.p).

(d) Check: $(^-1{\cdot}19)^2 - (3 \times {}^-1{\cdot}19) - 5 = {}^-0{\cdot}0139$ ✓

F Solving equations by iteration (2)

F1 (a)
$$x^2 + x - 5 = 0$$
Add 5 to both sides. $x^2 + x = 5$
Subtract x^2 from both sides. $x = 5 - x^2$

(b) The iteration formula does not give a converging sequence for any starting value.

F2 (a) 2, 2·236068, 2·1147425, 2·1745593, 2·1444423, 2·1594483, 2·1519322, 2·155687, 2·1538088, 2·1547477
Solution: 2·15 (to 2 d.p.)

(b) 2, 2·5, 1·6, 3·90625, 0·65536, 23·283064
The oscillations get larger.

F3 2, 2·1147425, 2·1444423, 2·1519322, 2·1538088
Solution: 2·15 (to 2 d.p.)

F4 (a) (1) 1·6, 1·5384615, 1·5757576, 1·5529412, 1·5668203, 1·5583483, 1·5635088, 1·5603614
This sequence converges.
Solution: 1·56 (to 2 d.p.)

(2) 1·6, 1·5, 1·6666667, 1·4, 1·8571429, 1·1538461, 2·4666667, 0·6216216
The oscillations get larger.

(b) (1) $^-$2·6, $^-$2·5, $^-$2·6666667, $^-$2·4, $^-$2·8571429, $^-$2·1538461, $^-$3·4666667, $^-$1·6216216
No convergence

(2) $^-$2·6, $^-$2·5384615, $^-$2·5757576, $^-$2·5529412, $^-$2·5668203, $^-$2·5583483, $^-$2·5635088, $^-$2·5603614, $^-$2·5622795, $^-$2·56111
This sequence converges.
Solution: $^-$2·56 (to 2 d.p.)

F5 1·45 and $^-$3·45 (to 2 d.p.)

F6

x	$^-6$	$^-5$	$^-4$	$^-3$	$^-2$	$^-1$	0	1	2
x^2+4x-9	3	$^-4$	$^-9$	$^-12$	$^-13$	$^-12$	$^-9$	$^-4$	3

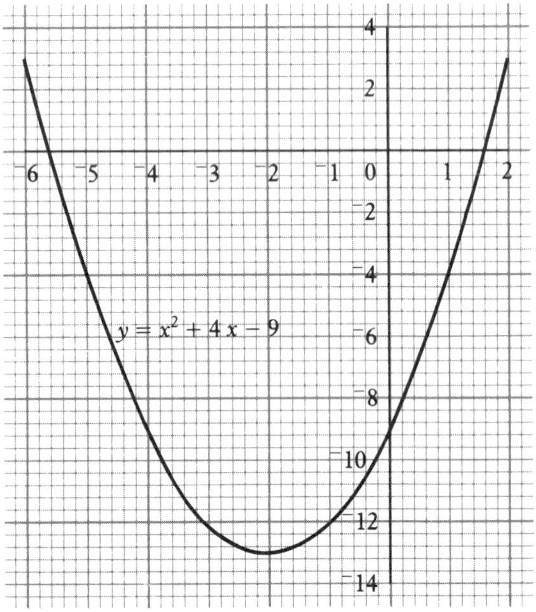

1·61 and $^-$5·61 (to 2 d.p.)

Money matters: saving and borrowing

Real information about savings schemes can be collected and schemes compared. In deciding on a scheme the advantage of a higher rate of interest has to be weighed against the disadvantages of some of the conditions relating to the scheme (for example, the saver may need to invest a minimum sum, or may need to give a month's notice of withdrawal).

Mortgages are of course a common instance of loans repaid in instalments, but are likely to be less real to pupils than hire purchase.

A Saving

A1 £95·28

A2 1·943% (to 4 s.f.)

B Borrowing

B1 He will take 5 years.

B2 £686·43

B3 (a) $£(1200 - I) \times 1{\cdot}2 = £(1440 - 1{\cdot}2I)$
(b) $£(1440 - 2{\cdot}2I)$
(c) $£(1440 - 2{\cdot}2I) \times 1{\cdot}2 = £(1728 - 2{\cdot}64I)$
(d) $1728 - 3{\cdot}64I = 0$
$I = 474{\cdot}73$ (to 2 d.p.)

B4 £32·30

B5 £4·26

B6 (a) £3·06 (b) 22%

B7 26%

B8 Loan A has an APR of 26%.
Loan B has an APR of 24%.
So B has the lower APR.

10 The sine and cosine functions (2)

Chapter 5 introduced the basic functions $\theta \rightarrow \sin\theta$ and $\theta \rightarrow \cos\theta$ and their graphs; this chapter looks at some other functions involving sine and cosine.

A Amplitude and period

A1 (a) 6 (b) $\theta \rightarrow 6\sin\theta$

A2 (a), (c)

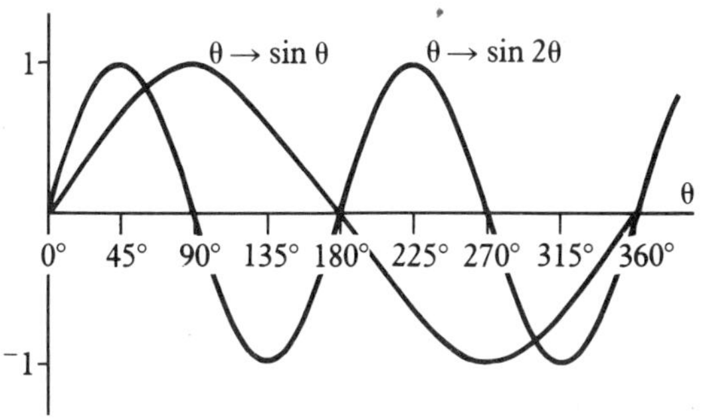

(b)

θ	0°	30°	60°	90°	120°	150°	180°
sin 2θ	0	0·87	0·87	0	$^{-}0{\cdot}87$	$^{-}0{\cdot}87$	0
θ	210°	240°	270°	300°	330°	360°	
sin 2θ	0·87	0·87	0	$^{-}0{\cdot}87$	$^{-}0{\cdot}87$	0	

(c) The period is 180°.

A3 (a) 120° (b) 4

A4 (a) Amplitude 5, period 180°
(b) Amplitude 10, period 120°
(c) Amplitude 20, period 720°

B The length of day

B1 About 14 hours

B2 (a) About 21 June
(b) About 21 December
(c) About 19 March, 25 September

B3 (a) 0·7 hour (b) 0·7 hour
(c) In the spring (d) In the autumn

B4 (a) 9·0 hours (b) 13·0 hours
(c) 15·8 hours (d) 7·5 hours
(all to 1 d.p.)
Compare with these figures from the table:
(a) 9·3 hours (b) 12·9 hours
(c) 15·5 hours (d) 7·5 hours

B5 (a) 8·4 hours (b) 8·9 hours (to 1 d.p.)

B6 Pupil's calculation of length of day at home on birthday

11 Inequalities

This chapter deals with the graphical representation of inequalities as regions, and of simultaneous inequalities as the overlap of regions. Although the questions in section C are somewhat artificial, being limited to two variables, they give an opportunity to practise the skill of translating from statements in words to algebraic statements.

A Regions

A1 (a) $x < 1$ (b) $x > {}^{-}2$ (c) $y > 2$
(d) $y < {}^{-}1$

A2 (a) 10·5, $2x + 3y > 10$ (b) 10, $2x + 3y = 10$
(c) 11·5, $2x + 3y > 10$ (d) 9·5, $2x + 3y < 10$
(e) 9·7, $2x + 3y < 10$

A3 (a) $2x - y < 4$ (b) $x + 3y > 9$ (c) $y > \frac{1}{2}x + 1$

A4

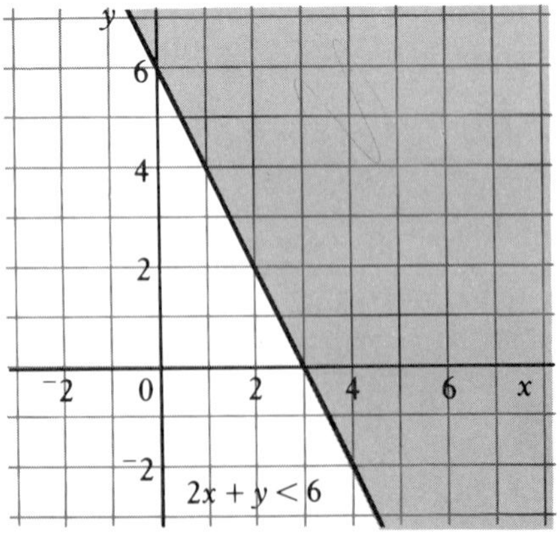

A5

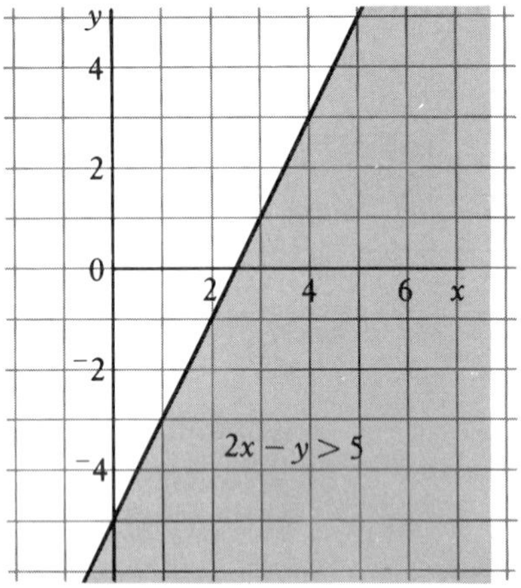

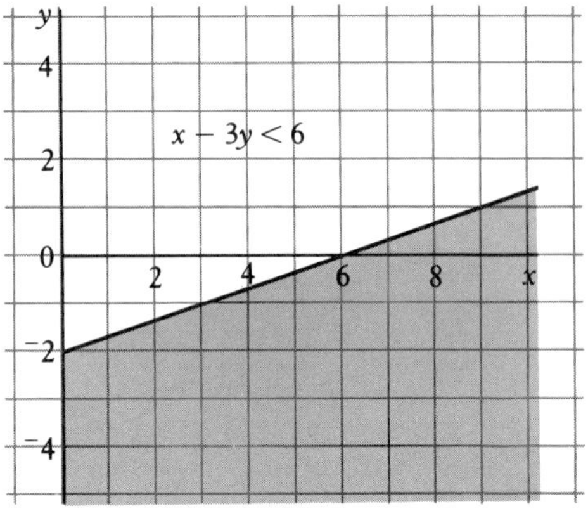

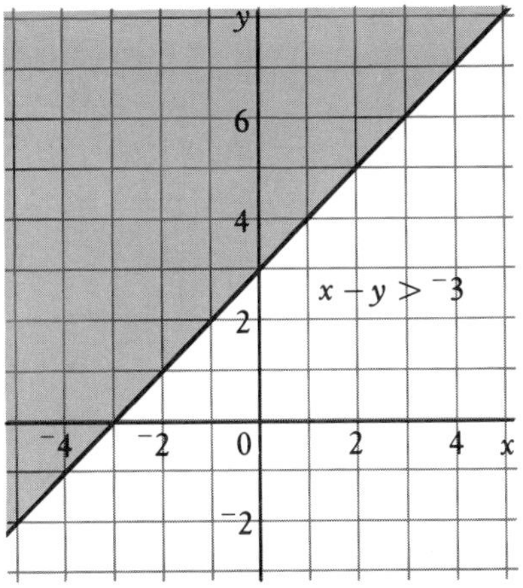

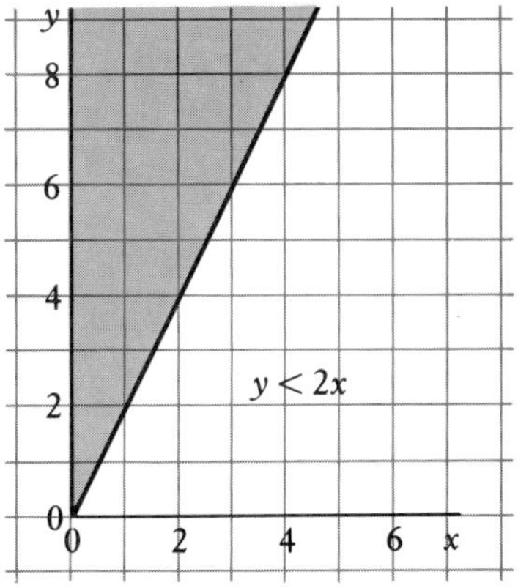

A6

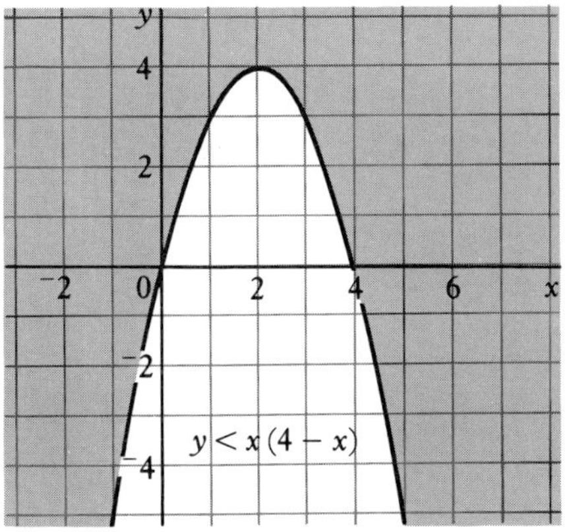

B Regions with two boundaries

B1 (a) $x + 2y > 8$ (b) $y > x + 2$
(c) $x + 2y > 8$ and $y > x + 2$

B2 (a) $5x + 3y > 15$ and $2x - 3y < 6$
(b) $y > x^2$ and $y < 5$
(c) $x + y < 6$ and $y < x$

B3

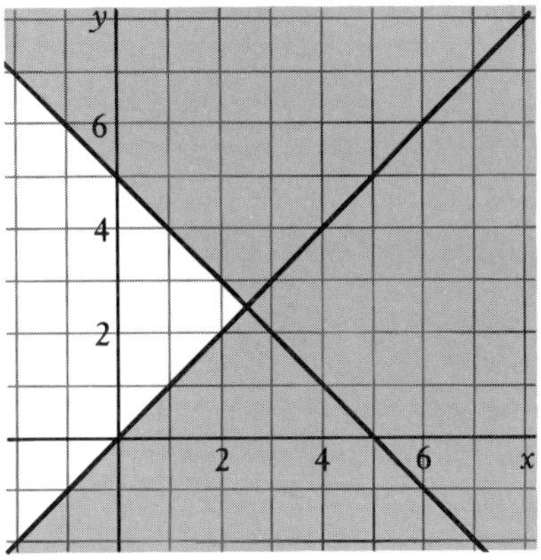

B4

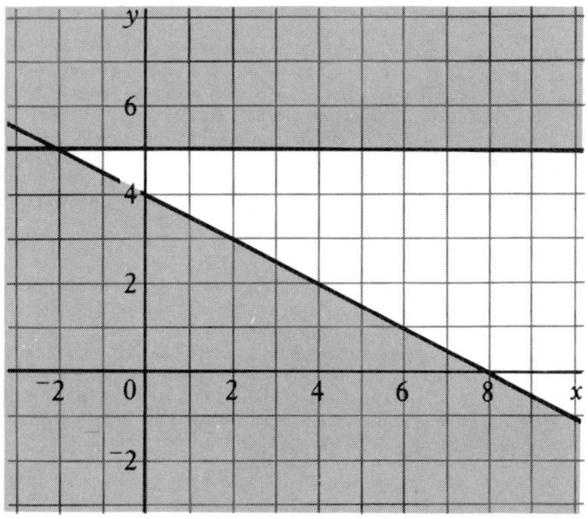

B5

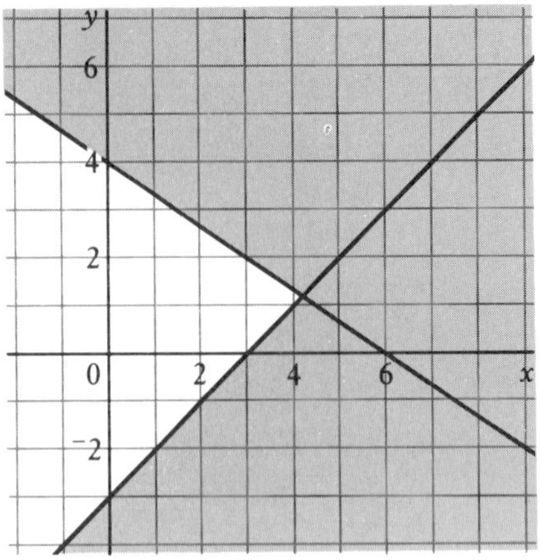

B6 A: $y > x - 1$ and $x + y > 4$
B: $y < x - 1$ and $x + y > 4$
C: $y < x - 1$ and $x + y < 4$
D: $y > x - 1$ and $x + y < 4$

B7

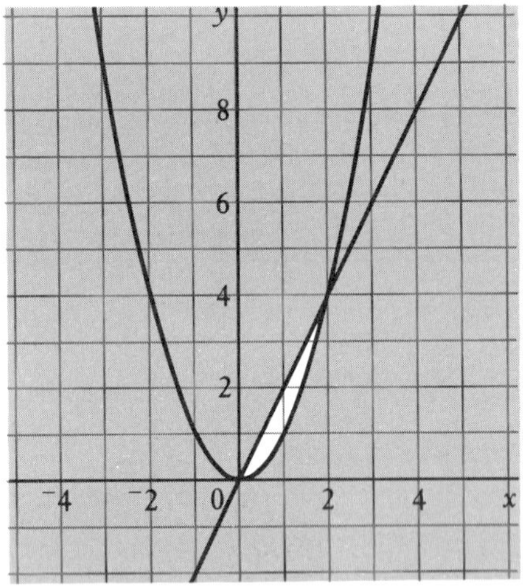

B8

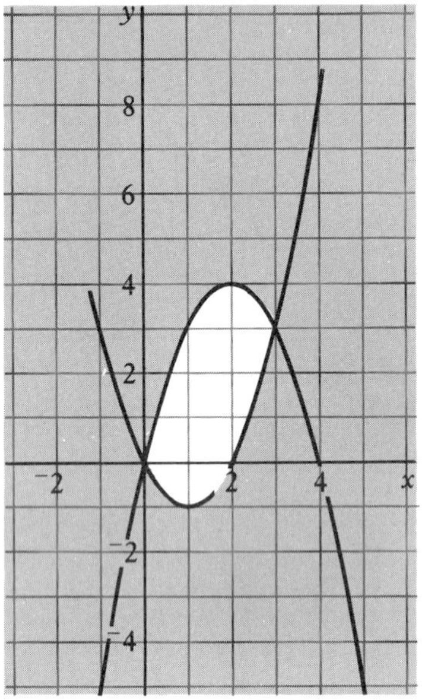

C Graphing constraints

C1

Trousers	**Skirts**	**Profit**
5	0	£80
4	2	£86
3	3	£81
2	5	£87
1	6	£82
0	7	£77

The most profitable combination is to make 2 pairs of trousers and 5 skirts.

C2 (a) $200x + 80y \leq 1000$
(c) $100x + 250y \leq 1000$
(b), (d), (e)

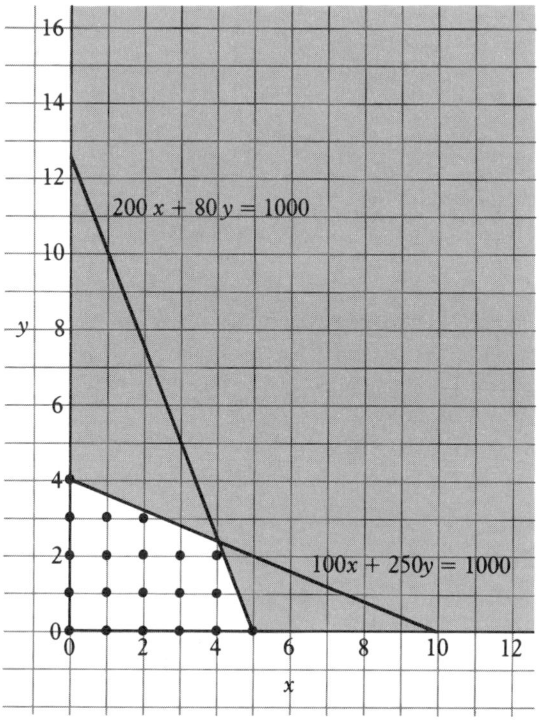

(f)

Jumpers	Cardigans	Profit
5	0	£50
4	2	£64
2	3	£56
0	4	£48

The most profitable combination is to make 4 jumpers and 2 cardigans.

C3 (a) $24x + 40y$ (b) $24x + 40y \geq 120$
(d) $50x + 80y$ (e) $50x + 80y \leq 400$

(c), (f)

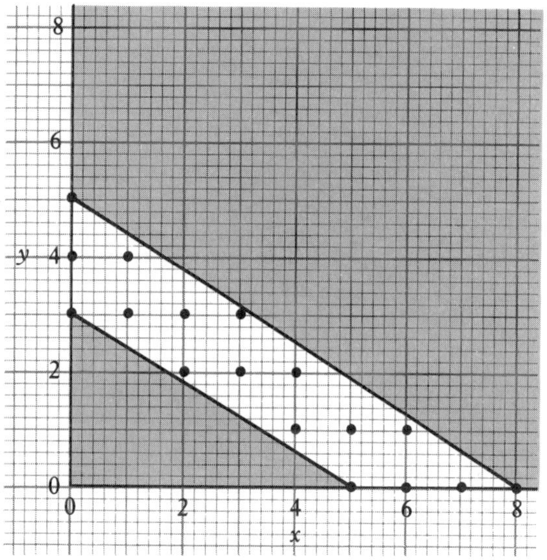

(g), (h), (i)

Small coaches	Large coaches	Cost	Number of children	Cost per child
8	0	£400	192	£2·08
7	0	£350	168	£2·08
6	0	£300	144	£2·08
6	1	£380	184	£2·07
5	0	£250	120	£2·08
5	1	£330	160	£2·06
4	1	£280	136	£2·06
4	2	£360	176	£2·05
3	2	£310	152	£2·04
3	3	£390	192	£2·03
2	2	£260	128	£2·03
2	3	£340	168	£2·02
1	3	£290	144	£2·01
1	4	£370	184	£2·01
0	3	£240	120	£2·00
0	4	£320	160	£2·00
0	5	£400	200	£2·00

The cheapest combination is 3 large coaches.
The combination which maximises the number of children that can be taken is 5 large coaches.
The combinations which give the cheapest cost per child are 5 large coaches, 4 large coaches, and 3 large coaches.

C4 (a) $20x + 16y \leq 160$ (b) $40x + 60y \leq 480$

(c)

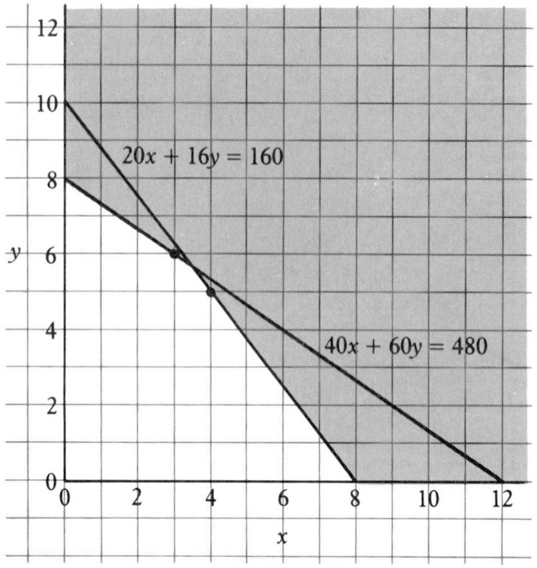

(d) 9 vehicles

---

12 Vector geometry

In all the work on vectors done so far, each vector has been specified numerically, either as a column vector or by giving its length and direction (bearing). In this chapter the vectors are not specified numerically, but are defined in relation to geometrical figures. The chief skill here is that of expressing one such vector as a combination of others.

A Displacement vectors

A1 (a) $\overrightarrow{BC}, \overrightarrow{CD}, \overrightarrow{EF}, \overrightarrow{FG}, \overrightarrow{GH}, \overrightarrow{IJ}, \overrightarrow{JK}, \overrightarrow{KL}, \overrightarrow{MN}, \overrightarrow{NO}, \overrightarrow{OP}$

(b) $\overrightarrow{BF}, \overrightarrow{CG}, \overrightarrow{DH}, \overrightarrow{EI}, \overrightarrow{FJ}, \overrightarrow{GK}, \overrightarrow{HL}, \overrightarrow{IM}, \overrightarrow{JN}, \overrightarrow{KO}, \overrightarrow{LP}$

A2 (a) Two of: $\overrightarrow{AI}, \overrightarrow{BJ}, \overrightarrow{CK}, \overrightarrow{DL}, \overrightarrow{EM}, \overrightarrow{FN}, \overrightarrow{GO}, \overrightarrow{HP}$

(b) Two of: $\overrightarrow{AD}, \overrightarrow{EH}, \overrightarrow{IL}, \overrightarrow{MP}$

A3 (a) Two of: $\overrightarrow{BA}, \overrightarrow{CB}, \overrightarrow{DC}, \overrightarrow{GF}, \overrightarrow{HG}, \overrightarrow{JI}, \overrightarrow{KJ}, \overrightarrow{LK}, \overrightarrow{NM}, \overrightarrow{ON}, \overrightarrow{PO}$

(b) Two of: $\overrightarrow{EA}, \overrightarrow{FB}, \overrightarrow{GC}, \overrightarrow{HD}, \overrightarrow{IE}, \overrightarrow{JF}, \overrightarrow{KG}, \overrightarrow{LH}, \overrightarrow{MI}, \overrightarrow{NJ}, \overrightarrow{OK}, \overrightarrow{PL}$

A4 (a) Two of: $\overrightarrow{CA}, \overrightarrow{DB}, \overrightarrow{HF}, \overrightarrow{KI}, \overrightarrow{LJ}, \overrightarrow{OM}, \overrightarrow{PN}$

(b) Two of: $\overrightarrow{MA}, \overrightarrow{NB}, \overrightarrow{OC}, \overrightarrow{PD}$

B Adding and subtracting vectors

B1 Diagrams of $\mathbf{a} + \mathbf{b}$, $2\mathbf{a} + \mathbf{b}$ and $2\mathbf{a} + 2\mathbf{b}$, using own choice of $\mathbf{a}$ and $\mathbf{b}$.

B2 Diagrams of $\mathbf{a} - \mathbf{b}$, $\mathbf{b} - \mathbf{a}$, $2\mathbf{a} - \mathbf{b}$ and $\mathbf{a} - 2\mathbf{b}$, using same choice of $\mathbf{a}$ and $\mathbf{b}$

B3 (a) $\overrightarrow{DC}$ (b) $\overrightarrow{AB}$ (c) $\overrightarrow{DA}$ and $\overrightarrow{CB}$

(d) $\overrightarrow{AD}$ and $\overrightarrow{BC}$

C Expressing vectors in terms of given vectors

C1 (a) $^{-}\mathbf{v}$ (b) $\mathbf{u} - \mathbf{v}$ (c) $^{-}2\mathbf{u}$
(d) $^{-}2\mathbf{u} - \mathbf{v}$ (e) $^{-}\mathbf{u} - \mathbf{v}$

C2 (a) $\mathbf{a} + \mathbf{b}$ (b) $\mathbf{b} - \mathbf{a}$ (c) $\mathbf{a} - \mathbf{b}$

C3 (a) $2\mathbf{u}$ (b) $^{-}2\mathbf{v}$ (c) $\mathbf{v} - \mathbf{u}$
(d) $2\mathbf{v} - 2\mathbf{u}$ (e) $2\mathbf{v} - \mathbf{u}$ (f) $\mathbf{v} - 2\mathbf{u}$

C4 (a) $2\mathbf{b}$ (b) $\frac{1}{2}\mathbf{a}$ (c) $\mathbf{a} + \mathbf{b}$
(d) $2\mathbf{b} - \mathbf{a}$ (e) $2\mathbf{b} + \frac{1}{2}\mathbf{a}$ (f) $\mathbf{b} - \frac{1}{2}\mathbf{a}$

C5 (a) $2\mathbf{u}$ (b) $2\mathbf{v}$ (c) $2\mathbf{u} - \mathbf{v}$
(d) $2\mathbf{v} - \mathbf{u}$ (e) $\mathbf{v} - \mathbf{u}$ (f) $2\mathbf{v} - 2\mathbf{u}$

D Proving by vectors

D1 (a) (i) $6\mathbf{a} + 2\mathbf{b}$ (ii) $3\mathbf{a} + \mathbf{b}$
(b) $^{-}4\mathbf{a} + 4\mathbf{b}$ (c) $^{-}\mathbf{a} + \mathbf{b}$
(d) $\overrightarrow{CF} = 4\overrightarrow{CH}$
(e) C, H and F lie on a straight line.

D2 (a) $2\mathbf{a} - 2\mathbf{b}$
(b) (i) $^{-}2\mathbf{a} + 6\mathbf{b}$ (ii) $^{-}\mathbf{a} + 3\mathbf{b}$
(iii) $\mathbf{a} + 3\mathbf{b}$ (iv) $\frac{1}{2}\mathbf{a} + 1\frac{1}{2}\mathbf{b}$
(v) $\frac{1}{2}\mathbf{a} - \frac{1}{2}\mathbf{b}$
(c) $\overrightarrow{DC} = 4\overrightarrow{DG}$
(d) D, G and C lie on a straight line.

D3 (a) $\overrightarrow{CF} = {}^{-}3\mathbf{a} + 6\mathbf{b}$, $\overrightarrow{CG} = {}^{-}\mathbf{a} + 2\mathbf{b}$
$\overrightarrow{EG} = 2\mathbf{a} - \mathbf{b}$, $\overrightarrow{ED} = 6\mathbf{a} - 3\mathbf{b}$
(b) $\overrightarrow{ED} = 3\overrightarrow{EG}$

E Position vectors

E1 (a) $\mathbf{a} + \mathbf{b}$ (b) $^{-}\mathbf{a} + \mathbf{b}$ (c) $^{-}\mathbf{a}$
(d) $^{-}\mathbf{a} - \mathbf{b}$ (e) $^{-}\mathbf{b}$ (f) $\mathbf{a} - \mathbf{b}$
(g) $\frac{1}{2}\mathbf{a} + \mathbf{b}$ (h) $\mathbf{a} - \frac{1}{2}\mathbf{b}$ (i) $^{-}\frac{1}{2}\mathbf{a} - \mathbf{b}$
(j) $\frac{1}{2}\mathbf{a} - \frac{1}{2}\mathbf{b}$

E2 B $\mathbf{a} + \mathbf{c}$, D $^{-}\mathbf{a}$, E $^{-}\mathbf{a} - \mathbf{c}$, F $^{-}\mathbf{c}$

E3 (a) $\mathbf{s} - \mathbf{r}$ (b) $\frac{1}{3}\mathbf{s} - \frac{1}{3}\mathbf{r}$
(c) $\frac{2}{3}\mathbf{r} + \frac{1}{3}\mathbf{s}$

E4 (a) $\mathbf{b} - \mathbf{a}$ (b) $\frac{3}{4}\mathbf{b} - \frac{3}{4}\mathbf{a}$
(c) $\frac{1}{4}\mathbf{a} + \frac{3}{4}\mathbf{b}$

E5 (a)

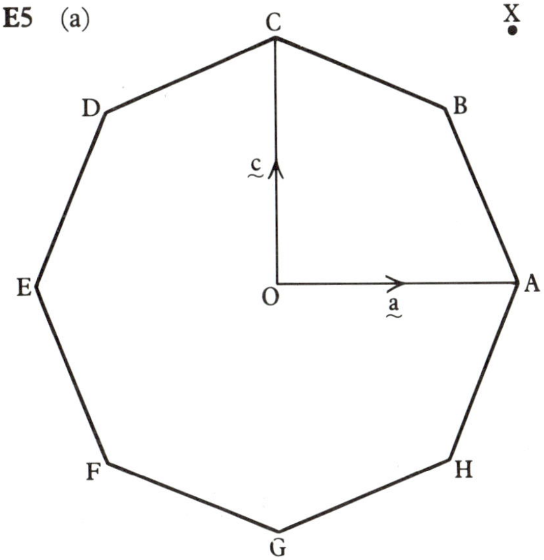

(b) $\sqrt{2}$ units (1·414 units to 3 d.p.)
(c) Length of OB = 1 unit, so
$\overrightarrow{OB} = \frac{1}{\sqrt{2}}(\mathbf{a} + \mathbf{c}) = 0{\cdot}707\,(\mathbf{a} + \mathbf{c})$ (to 3 d.p.)
(d) D $0{\cdot}707(\mathbf{c} - \mathbf{a})$, E $^{-}\mathbf{a}$, F $^{-}0{\cdot}707(\mathbf{a} + \mathbf{c})$,
G $^{-}\mathbf{c}$, H $0{\cdot}707(\mathbf{a} - \mathbf{c})$

E6 (a) $\frac{1}{2}(\mathbf{a} + \mathbf{b})$ (b) $\mathbf{b} - \frac{1}{2}\mathbf{a}$ (c) $\frac{1}{2}\mathbf{b} - \frac{1}{2}\mathbf{a}$
(d) $^{-}\frac{1}{2}(\mathbf{a} + \mathbf{b})$ (e) $\frac{1}{2}\mathbf{a} - \mathbf{b}$ (f) $\mathbf{a} - \frac{1}{2}\mathbf{b}$

Review 3

9 Iteration

9.1 (a) 0, 0·2, 0·24, 0·248, 0·2496, 0·24992, 0·249984, 0·2499968
(b) 0·25
(c) When $s_1 = 0{\cdot}25$, $s_2 = \frac{1{\cdot}25}{5} = 0{\cdot}25$ ✓

9.2 (a) 3·5 (b) $^{-}4$ and 1

9.3 (a) 0, 1, 1·4142136, 1·553774, 1·5980532, 1·6118478, 1·6161212, 1·6174428, 1·6178513
(b) 1·62 (to 2 d.p.)

9·4 (a)

x	$^{-}2$	$^{-}1$	0	1	2	3	4	5
$x(x-3)$	10	4	0	$^{-}2$	$^{-}2$	0	4	10

(b)

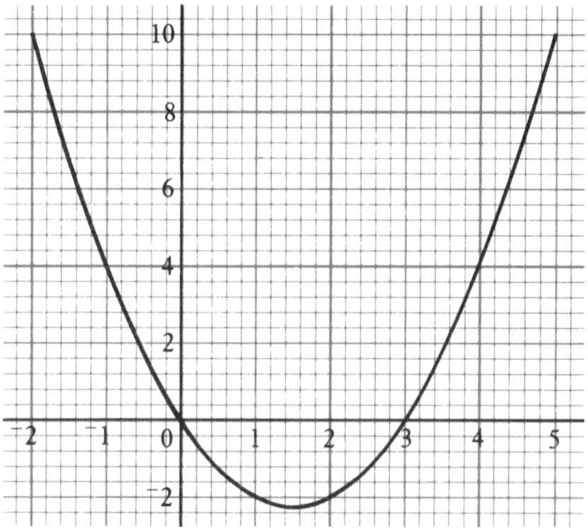

(c) About $^{-}0{\cdot}3$ and $3{\cdot}3$

(d) $^{-}0{\cdot}30$ and $3{\cdot}30$ (to 2 d.p.)

10 The sine and cosine functions (2)

10.1 $\theta \to \sin 2\theta$

10.2 $\theta \to 2\cos\theta$

11 Inequalities

11.1

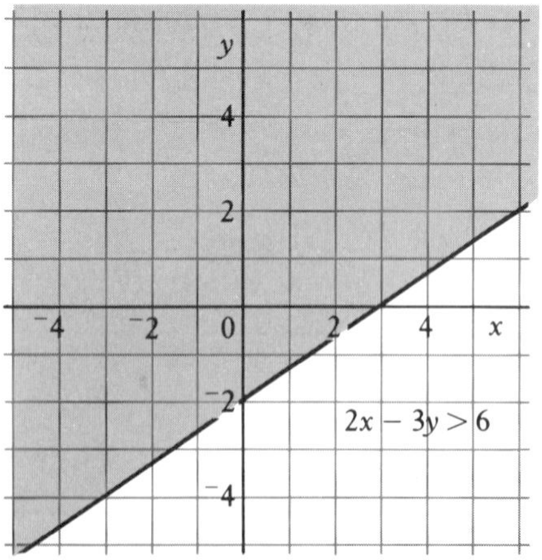

11.2 (a) $y > {}^{-}1$ (b) $y < \frac{1}{2}x$

11.3 $5x + 4y > 20$ and $x - y < 2$

11.4

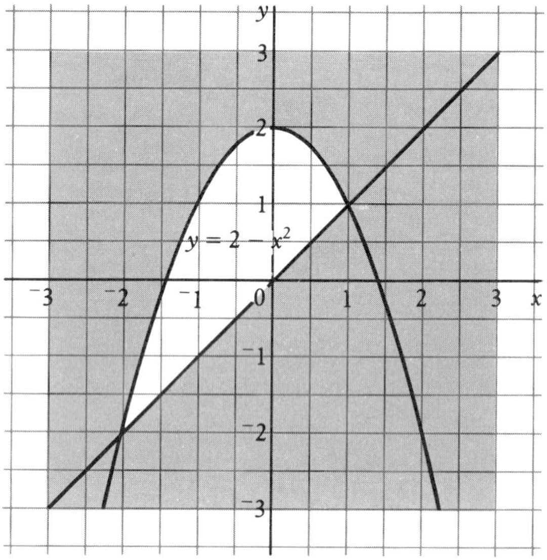

11.5 (a) $120x + 240y \leq 21600$ so $x + 2y \leq 180$

(b) $y \geq 40$, $x + y \geq 105$, $y \geq \frac{1}{2}x$

(c)

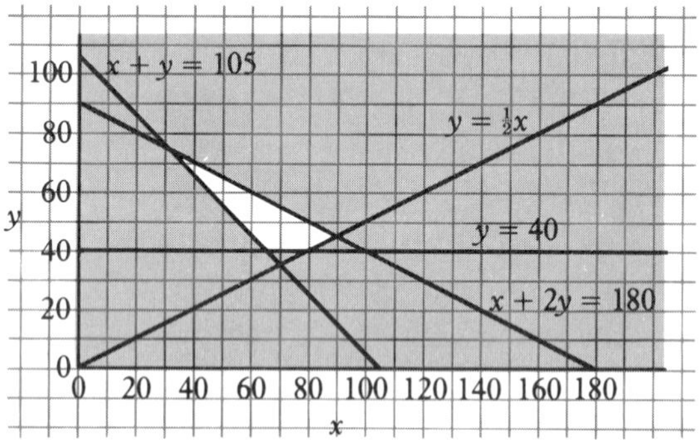

(d) From 30 to 90 unskilled workers

12 Vector geometry

12.1 (a) $\mathbf{r} + \mathbf{s}$ (b) $2\mathbf{r}$ (c) $\mathbf{s} - \mathbf{r}$ (d) $\mathbf{s} - 2\mathbf{r}$

12.2 (a) $\mathbf{a} + \mathbf{b}$ (b) $\mathbf{a} + \frac{1}{2}\mathbf{b}$ (c) $\frac{1}{2}\mathbf{a} + \mathbf{b}$
(d) $^{-}\frac{1}{2}\mathbf{a}$ (e) $\mathbf{b} - \frac{1}{2}\mathbf{a}$ (f) $\frac{1}{2}\mathbf{b} - \mathbf{a}$
(g) $\frac{1}{2}\mathbf{a} - \frac{1}{2}\mathbf{b}$ (h) $^{-}\frac{1}{2}\mathbf{a} - \mathbf{b}$

12.3 (a) $2\mathbf{u}$ (b) $\mathbf{v} - \mathbf{u}$ (c) $\mathbf{u} + \mathbf{v}$
(d) $\frac{1}{2}\mathbf{u} + \frac{1}{2}\mathbf{v}$ (e) $\frac{1}{2}\mathbf{v} - 1\frac{1}{2}\mathbf{u}$
(f) $\frac{1}{2}\mathbf{v} - \frac{1}{2}\mathbf{u}$

12.4 (a) $^{-}2\mathbf{a} + 2\mathbf{b}$
(b) (i) $3\mathbf{a} + \mathbf{b}$ (ii) $1\frac{1}{2}\mathbf{a} + \frac{1}{2}\mathbf{b}$
(iii) $\frac{1}{2}\mathbf{b} - \frac{1}{2}\mathbf{a}$
(c) $\overrightarrow{CE} = 2\mathbf{b} - 2\mathbf{a} = 4(\frac{1}{2}\mathbf{b} - \frac{1}{2}\mathbf{a}) = 4\overrightarrow{CH}$
Points C, H and E lie on a straight line.

12.5 (a) $2\mathbf{a} + \mathbf{e}$ (b) $2\mathbf{a} + 2\mathbf{e}$ (c) $\mathbf{a} + 2\mathbf{e}$
(d) $1\frac{1}{2}\mathbf{a} + \frac{1}{2}\mathbf{e}$ (e) $2\mathbf{a} + 1\frac{1}{2}\mathbf{e}$

General review

Sections 1 to 27 give an opportunity for topic-by-topic revision, which may reveal areas of weakness where further attention is necessary. Section M is made up of questions taken from the pilot 16+ examination based on the SMP 11–16 course. Questions M1 to M14 appeared on paper 3 and questions M15 to M38 on paper 4 (although not all on the same occasion in either case).

1 Whole numbers and decimals

1.1 You could buy (a).

1.2 (a) £5·44 (b) £1·53 (c) £42·16

1.3 (a) 0·833 kg (to 3 d.p.) (b) 1·2 kg

1.4 Standard cup: 10 ml costs 1·58p.
Large beaker: 10 ml costs 1·67p.
The standard cup is better value.

1.5 832 labels

1.6 40 doses

1.7 (a) 37·89 (b) 38 (c) 0·0399
(d) 363 000

1.8 (a) 2×10^{7} (b) 8×10^{-5}
(c) $3{\cdot}62 \times 10^{6}$ (d) $9{\cdot}27 \times 10^{-6}$

1.9 (a) Minimum 11·52, maximum 12·5
(b) Minimum 0·48, maximum 0·52 (to 2 d.p.)

1.10 (a) Minimum 499·95 m, maximum 500·05 m
(b) Minimum 4·575 s, maximum 4·585 s
(c) Minimum 109·04 m/s, maximum 109·30 m/s

2 Percentage

2.1 (a) £126 (b) £1·40

2.2 (a) 36·0% (b) 10·9%
(c) 26·7% (d) 54·8%
(all to nearest 0·1%)

2.3 (a) £9499 (b) 14·0% (to nearest 0·1%)

2.4 (a) 8% (b) 4% (c) 27%

2.5 (a) 1·07 (b) 19·84%

2.6 Lower. The sale price is $1{\cdot}16 \times 0{\cdot}85 = 0{\cdot}986$ times the original price.

2.7 No, the newspaper conclusion is not sensible because 67% of the men caught flu, but only 63% of the women.

3 Fractions

3.1 $\frac{1}{2}''$, $\frac{5}{8}''$, $\frac{11}{16}''$, $\frac{3}{4}''$, $\frac{15}{16}''$

3.2 $\frac{13}{16}''$

3.3 (a) 6·4 mm (b) 19·1 mm (c) 15·9 mm
(d) 20·6 mm

3.4 $\frac{3}{10}$

4 Ratio

4.1 (a) A 1·33, B 2·04, C 1·5, D 1·5
(b) Screens C and D

4.2 (a) 2·13 (b) 0·470 (c) 0·728

4.3 (a) 3·90 cm (b) 8·31 cm (both to 3 s.f.)

4.4 37·5%

5 Gradient

5.1 (a) 0·4 (b) 1·5 (c) 0·714 (to 3 s.f.)

5.2 Gradient of P 0·138
Gradient of Q 0·128
Hill P is steeper.

5.3 (a) $^{-}0{\cdot}5$ (b) 0·2 (c) $^{-}0{\cdot}75$

6 Rates

6.1 (a) 4·8 litres/min (b) 3·24 min (to 3 s.f.)

6.2

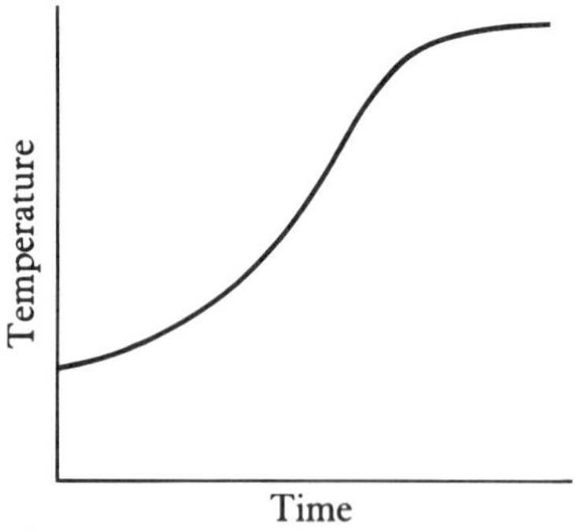

6.3 (a) 442 m.p.h. (b) 3·55 hours
(both to 3 s.f.)

6.4 (a) (i) 76 m.p.h. (ii) 72 m.p.h.
(iii) 68 m.p.h.
(b) 72·9 m.p.h.

6.5 (a) 0·300 g (b) 0·588 litre
(both to 3 s.f.)

6.6 (a) 40 litres/min (b) 24 litres/min

6.7 No. She has enough fuel for 368 miles more, assuming the consumption rate remains the same.

7 Constructing formulas

7.1 (a) 42 (b) $2n + 2$ (c) $\frac{1}{2}(p - 2)$

7.2 (a) $nw + b$ (b) $\dfrac{f - e}{n}$

7.3 £$(\dfrac{a}{n} - 1)$

7.4 (a) $4n$ (b) $(n - 1)^2$

7.5 (a) $170a + 410b$ grams
(b) $25a + 54b$ pence
(c) $500 - 25a - 54b$ pence

7.6 (a) $\dfrac{x}{y}$ litres/min (b) $\dfrac{x}{60y}$ litres/second
(c) $\dfrac{60x}{y}$ litres

8 Techniques of algebra

8.1 (a) 19 (b) 11 (c) 20 (d) 25
(e) 13 (f) 1 (g) 16 (h) 1
(i) $^{-}0{\cdot}5$ (j) $^{-}5$

8.2 (a) 49 (b) 0·81 (c) 42·25

8.3 (a) $p(qr + p) = 46$ (b) $p(q + qr) = 48$
(c) $(p + qp)^2 = 64$ (d) $q + qr^2 = 150$
(e) $(2q)^2 + r = 43$ (f) $(pr + q)p^2 = 68$

8.4 (a) 3·2 (b) 0·1 (c) 6·1 (d) 10.4
(e) 11·5

8.5 (a) 47 or $4{\cdot}7 \times 10^1$ (b) $9{\cdot}1 \times 10^{-12}$
(c) $1{\cdot}7 \times 10^{-8}$ (d) $2{\cdot}8 \times 10^9$
(e) $1{\cdot}9 \times 10^2$ (f) $5{\cdot}2 \times 10^{-3}$

8.6 (a) $3p + 3q$ (b) $3p + 6q$ (c) $5a - 15$
(d) $ab - a^2$ (e) $x^2y + xy^2$

8.7 (a) $n + 7$ (b) $^{-}7x - 7y$ (c) $^{-}2a - 5$
(d) cannot be simplified. (e) $2u - 7$
(f) $5 + 4x$ (g) cannot be simplified.
(h) $8ab + a^2$

8.8 (a) $2x + 5$ (b) $x + 4$ (c) $13 - 2x$
(d) $5x + 8$ (e) $3x - 6$ (f) $5a$
(g) $5 + 12x$ (h) $2p^2 - pq$ (i) $4x - 13$

8.9 (a) $3(a + 2b)$ (b) $4(a - 3)$
(c) $b(ab + 5)$ (d) $2a(4b - a)$
(e) $pq(p - q)$

8.10 (a) $xy + 5x + 3y + 15$ (b) $2x^2 + 11x + 5$
(c) $6x^2 - 11x - 10$ (d) $9x^2 - 24x + 16$
(e) $25x^2 - 4$ (f) $16 - 40x + 25x^2$

8.11 (a) $(x + 3)(x + 4)$ (b) $(x + 3)(x - 5)$
(c) $(x - 4)(x + 5)$ (d) $(x - 2)(x - 4)$

8.12 (a) $\frac{ac}{bd}$ (b) $\frac{4}{y}$ (c) $\frac{2x + 2y}{3x}$
(d) $\frac{3a}{2b}$ (e) $\frac{4a}{b}$

8.13 (a) $\frac{5b + 2a}{ab}$ (b) $\frac{rt - 2r}{st}$ (c) $\frac{ax - 3y}{3a^2}$
(d) $\frac{8x - 6}{x(x - 2)}$ (e) $\frac{5x^2 - 3}{x}$

9 Solving equations and manipulating formulas

9.1 (a) 15 (b) 7 (c) $^-4$
(d) $^-3$ (e) 2 (f) 3

9.2 (a) 10 (b) 3 (c) 1·5

9.3 (a) 3·90 (b) 0·43 (c) 0·45 (d) 6·25

9.4 (a) $P = \frac{RT}{V}$ (b) $V = \frac{RT}{P}$ (c) $R = \frac{PV}{T}$

9.5 (a) $u = mv$ (b) $v = \frac{u}{m}$

9.6 (a) 7 (b) 2·5 (c) $c = d - ab$
(d) $a = \frac{(d - c)}{b}$

9.7 (a) 126 (b) $^-24$ (c) $p = q(r + s)$
(d) $s = \frac{p}{q} - r$

9.8 (a) $5x$
(b) Gladys $x + 6$, Albert $5x + 6$
(c) $5x + 6 = 2(x + 6)$
Gladys is 2 years old.

9.9 Mark has £7·50.

9.10 (a) 1·8 (b) $^-1$ (c) 8

9.11 (a) 3·6 (b) $^-1$

9.12 (a) $r = \frac{ap}{qs}$ (b) $f = \frac{(e - d)}{s}$ (c) $a = \frac{2A}{h} - b$
(d) $r = \frac{(b - a)}{at}$ (e) $v = \sqrt{(ar)}$ (f) $u = \frac{t^2}{a}$
(g) $n = (ma)^2$ (h) $x = \frac{a}{y^2}$

9.13 (a) $P = \frac{V^2}{R}$ (b) $I = \frac{P}{V}$
(c) $V = \sqrt{(PR)}$ (d) $R = \frac{V^2}{P}$

9.14 $x = 6a + 7b - 6$

9.15 $A = \frac{C^2}{4\pi}$

9.16 $(x + 2)(x + 3)$
Solutions: $x = {}^-2$ or $x = {}^-3$

9.17 (a) $^-2$ or 4 (b) $^-6$ or 5 (c) 0 or 5
(d) $^-4$ or 1 (e) 3 or 5 (f) $^-10$ or 2

9.18 (a) About 2·3 (b) 2·32

9.19 (a) $2{\cdot}6^2 - 2{\cdot}6 - 4 = 0{\cdot}16$
(b) 2·56

10 Linear equations and inequalities

10.1 (a), (d)

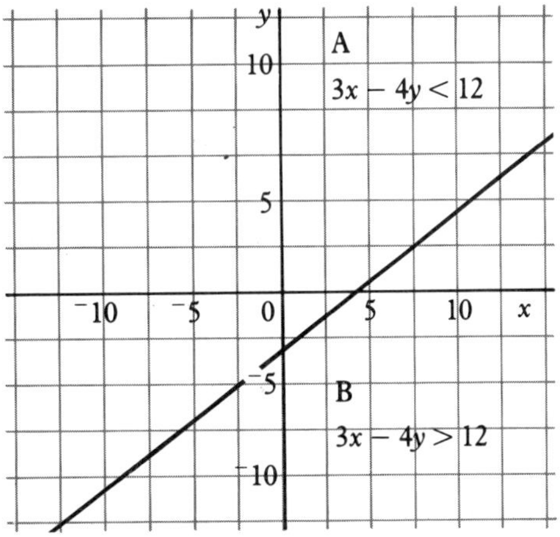

(b) $^-5$ (c) 21
(e) Region A

10.2 (a) £$(10x + 0{\cdot}03y)$
(b) $10x + 0{\cdot}03y \leq 90$
(c)

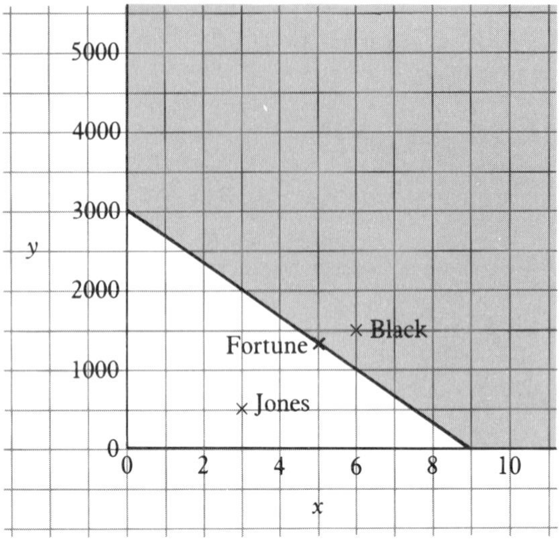

(d) (i) Yes (ii) No (iii) No

10.3 (a) 32 (b) 39 (c) 23 (d) 15

10.4 (a) 37 (b) 18·5 (c) 54 (d) 35

10.5 (a) $a = 14$, $b = 9$ (b) $a = 4$, $b = {}^{-}5$
(c) $x = 7$, $y = 3$ (d) $p = 10$, $q = 1$

10.6 Children £1·50, adults £2·50

10.7 A (6, 3), B (1, $^{-}2$), C (8, 2)

10.8 (a) No solution
(b) Infinite number of solutions

10.9

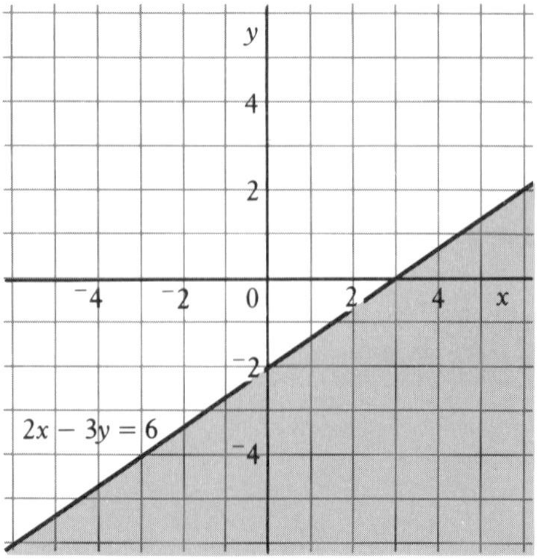

10.10 (a) $3x + 4y > 24$ and $x - 2y < 4$
(b) (6·4, 1·2)

11 Graphs and functions

11.1

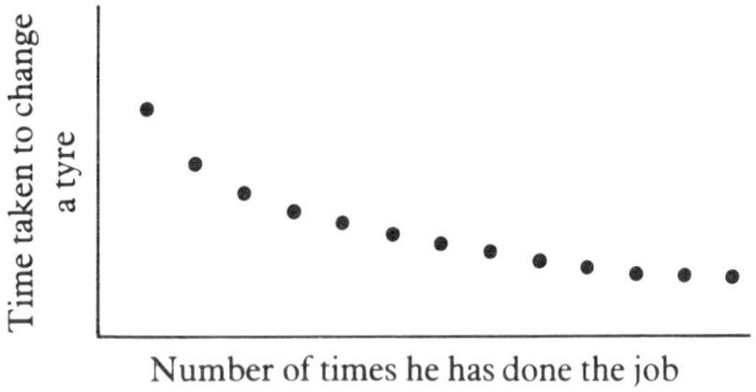

11.2 (a) AB, CD and FG – the car uses petrol at a higher rate in town driving, and these three sections of the graph are the steepest.
(b) The car was re-fuelled.

11.3 (a)

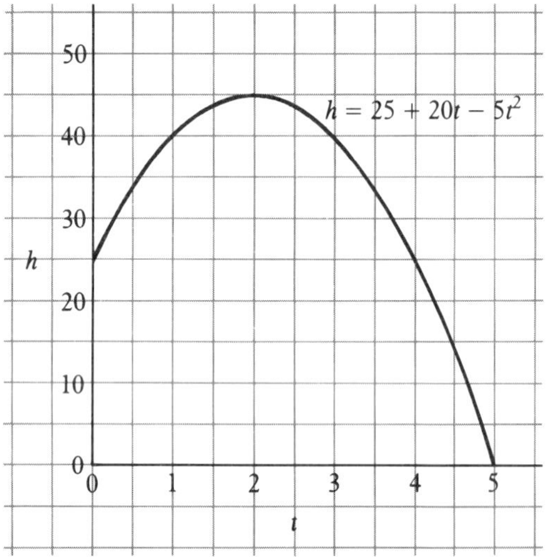

(b) About 3·5 seconds

11.4 (a) (i) 2 (ii) 3 (iii) $y = 2x + 3$
(b) (i) $^{-}\frac{1}{2}$ (ii) 3 (iii) $y = {}^{-}\frac{1}{2}x + 3$
(c) (i) $\frac{1}{2}$ (ii) $^{-}2$ (iii) $y = \frac{1}{2}x - 2$

11.5 (a), (b)

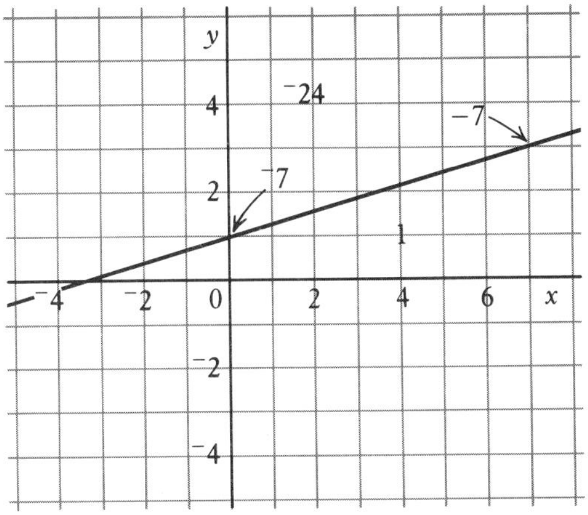

(c) $\frac{2}{7}$ (d) 1 (e) $y = \frac{2}{7}x + 1$

(f) Pupil's check

11.6 (a)

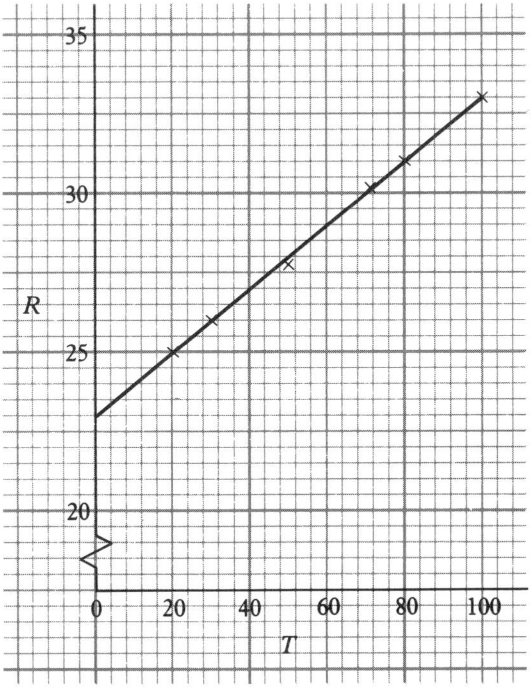

(b) Gradient 0·1, intercept 23

(c) $R = 0{\cdot}1T + 23$

11.7 (a) (i) $^-4$ (ii) 5 (iii) 17

(b) $^-5$ (c) 1·25

11.8 (a)

x	$(x+1)$		$(x-5)$	t(x)
$^-3$	$^-2$	×	$^-8$	16
$^-2$	$^-1$	×	$^-7$	7
$^-1$	0	×	$^-6$	0
0	1	×	$^-5$	$^-5$
1	2	×	$^-4$	$^-8$
2	3	×	$^-3$	$^-9$
3	4	×	$^-2$	$^-8$
4	5	×	$^-1$	$^-5$
5	6	×	0	0
6	7	×	1	7
7	8	×	2	16

(b)

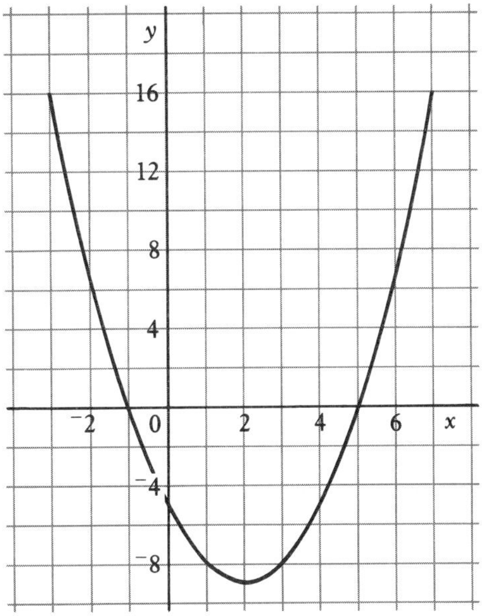

(c) Between about $^-1{\cdot}7$ and 5·7

(d) $x = {}^-1$ and $x = 5$

(e) Pupil's own explanation

11.9 At $x = 2$ and $x = 6$

11.10 (a) At $x = 0$ and $x = 4$

(b) At $x = {}^-3$ and $x = {}^-10$

(c) At $x = 1$ and $x = 5$

11.11 (a) C (b) B (c) A (d) E

11.12 (a)

$\sqrt{p}$	0·89	1·34	1·52	1·90	2·35	2·98
q	14·5	16·7	17·6	19·5	21·7	24·9

(b)

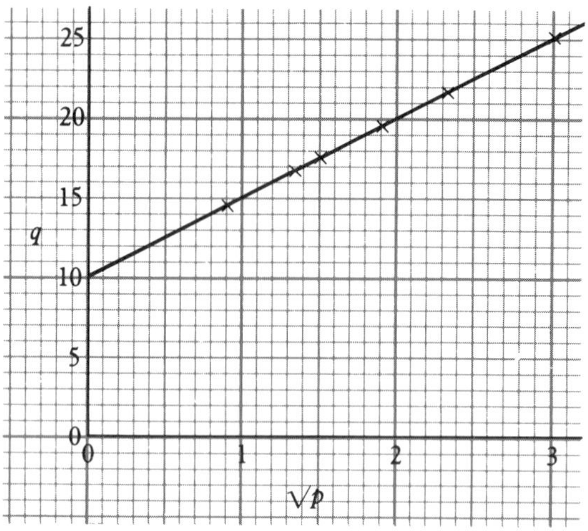

$a = 5,\ b = 10$ (approx.)

11.13

r^2	0·36	1·21	2·25	4·0	5·29	6·25
s	17·5	16·2	14·6	12·0	10·1	8·6

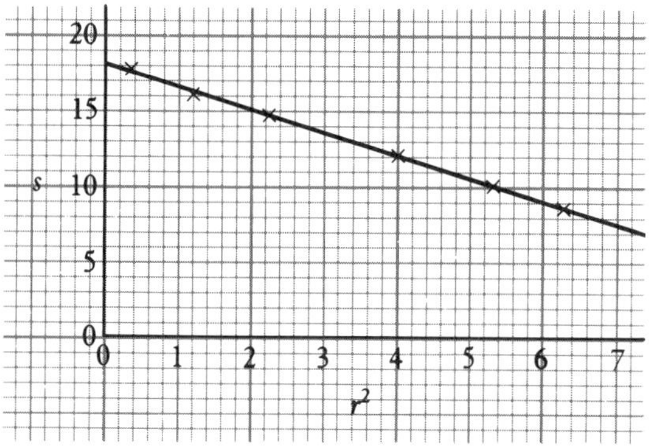

$a = {}^{-}1{\cdot}5,\ b = 18$ (approx.)

11.14 About 105 m
Pupil's explanation of method used to find area under graph

12 Proportionality

12.1 (a) (i) £3·00 (ii) £0·75 (iii) £2·25
(b) (i) 200 cm (ii) 100 cm (iii) 1000 cm

12.2 (a) 1·293 (to 4 s.f.) (b) 42·0 m

12.3 (a) 417 g (to nearest g), 80p (b) 625 cm

12.4 Containers C and F

12.5 (a)

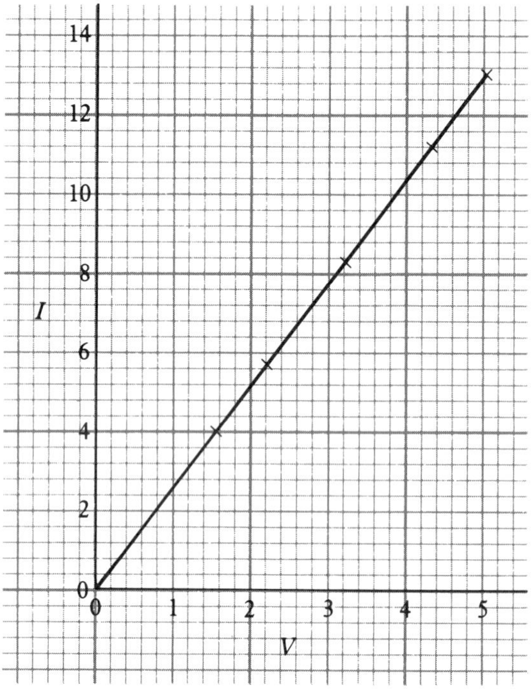

(b) Yes, the graph is a straight line through the origin.
(c) 2·6 (d) $I = 2{\cdot}6V$

12.6 (a) $y = 1{\cdot}4x$ (b) $y = 0{\cdot}8x$ (c) $y = 0{\cdot}5x$
(d) $y = 0{\cdot}2x$ (e) $y = 0{\cdot}125x$

12.7 (a) 54 m.p.h. (b) $19\frac{1}{2}$ hours

12.8 (a) 3·2 (b) 1 (c) 16

12.9 (a) 8400 (b) 1700

13 Exponential growth and decay

13.1 £199·80

13.2 (a)

t	0	1	2	3	4
T	215	65	27·5	18·125	15·78

(b)

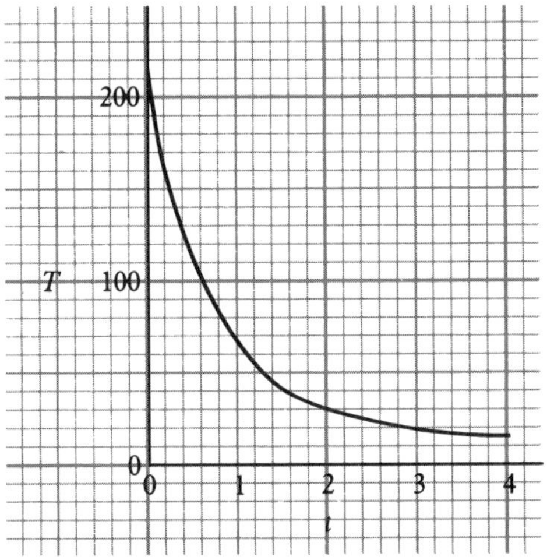

T gets closer and closer to 15.

14 Sequences and iteration

14.1 (a) 1, 3, 6, 10, 15, 21
(b) The triangle numbers

14.2 $a_n = 4n - 1$

14.3 (a) 17 (b) $u_n = 6n - 1$

14.4 $6n - 4$

14.5 $3 \times 4^{n+1}$

14.6 (a) 2, 9, 44, 219, 1094, 5469
(b) $d_{n+1} = 5d_n - 1$

14.7 19, 41, 85, 173

14.8 $a = 3,\ b = {}^{-}1$

14.9 (a) $r_{n+1} = r_n + 8$ (b) $r_n = 8n - 4$

14.10 (a) 8, 12·5, 19·25, 29·375
(b) No (c) $^{-}1$

14.11 (a) 0·8, 0·68, 0·608, 0·5648
(b) Possibly, but more terms are needed.
(c) 0·5

14.12 (a) $x = \dfrac{3}{x-2}$, so $x(x-2) = 3$
so $x^2 - 2x - 3 = 0$
(b) $x = {}^{-}1$ or $x = 3$

14.13 (a) $x^2 - x - 1 = 0$
so $x^2 - x = 1$
so $x(x-1) = 1$
so $x = \dfrac{1}{x-1}$
(b) 1·6, 1·6666667, 1·5, 2, 1, $^{-}$3333333·3
This sequence does not converge.
$^{-}$0·6, $^{-}$0·625, $^{-}$0·6153846, $^{-}$0·6190476, $^{-}$0·617647, $^{-}$0·6181818, $^{-}$0·6179775
This sequence converges to $^{-}$0·62 (to 2 d.p.).
One of the solutions is $^{-}$0·62 (to 2 d.p.).
(c) $x = \sqrt{(x+1)}$
$u_{n+1} = \sqrt{(u_n + 1)}$
1·6, 1·6124515, 1·616308, 1·6175005, 1·6178691, 1·617983
This sequence converges to 1·62 (to 2 d.p.), so this is the other solution.

15 Loci

15.1

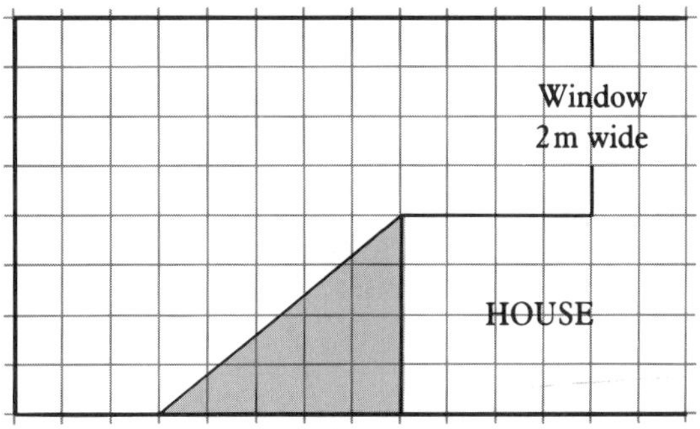

15.2

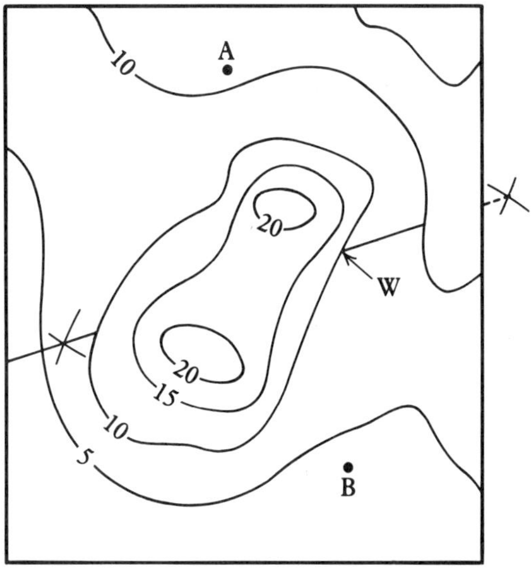

15.3

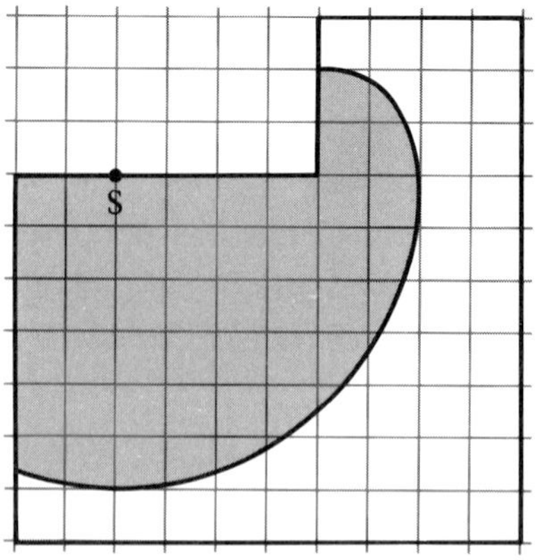

15.4

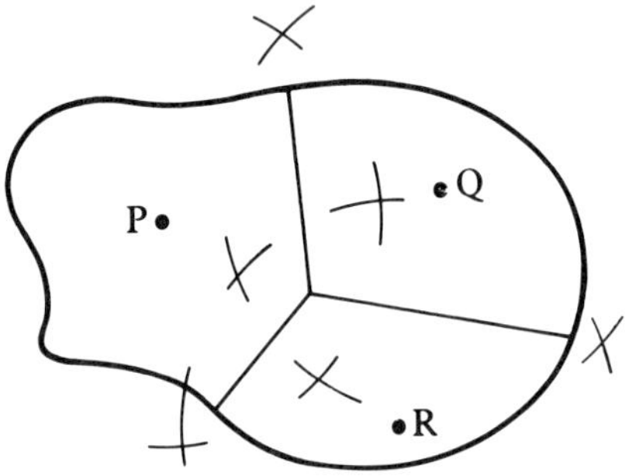

School P serves the largest area.

16 Pythagoras' rule

16.1 20·4 cm (to 3 s.f.)

16.2 (a) 6·71 (b) 6·40 (c) 8·25
(all to 3 s.f.)

17 The circle: circumference and area

17.1 (a) 30 cars (b) About 5 m
(c) About 150 m (d) About 50 m

17.2 (a) $135\,\text{m}^2$ (b) 18·4 m
(c) 0·520 m (d) $14{\cdot}9\,\text{m}^2$

17.3 (a) 33 000 cm (to 3 s.f.) (b) 550 cm/s

18 Angle relationships

18.1 $a = 71°$, $b = 88°$

18.2 $x = 31°$
Pupil's explanation of calculation is required.

18.3

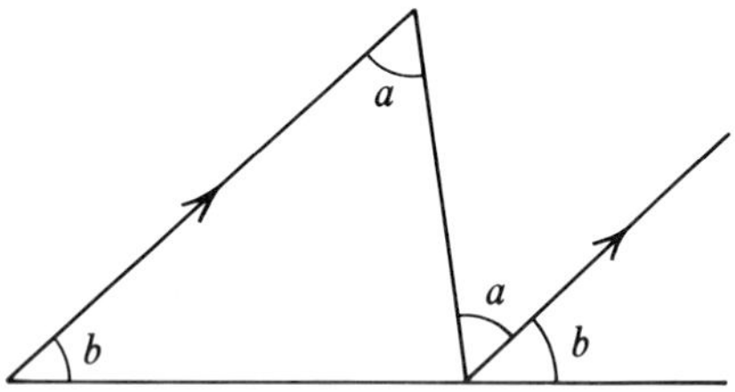

The angles marked a are equal (alternate angles).
The angles marked b are equal (corresponding angles).
So $x = a + b$.

18.4

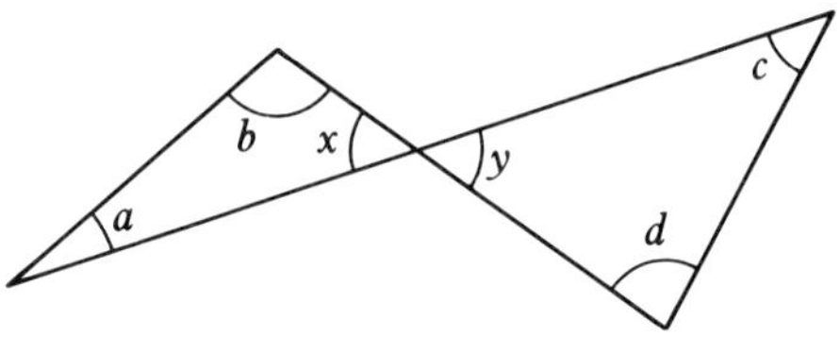

$x + a + b = 180°$ (angles in a triangle)
$y + c + d = 180°$ (angles in a triangle)
But $x = y$ (vertically opposite angles)
so $a + b = c + d$

18.5 18 sides

18.6 $x = 92°$
Pupil's explanation of calculation is required.

19 Mappings and symmetry

19.1 (a), (b), (d), (f) and (h) have 2-fold rotation centres.

19.2 Some possible ways are shown below:

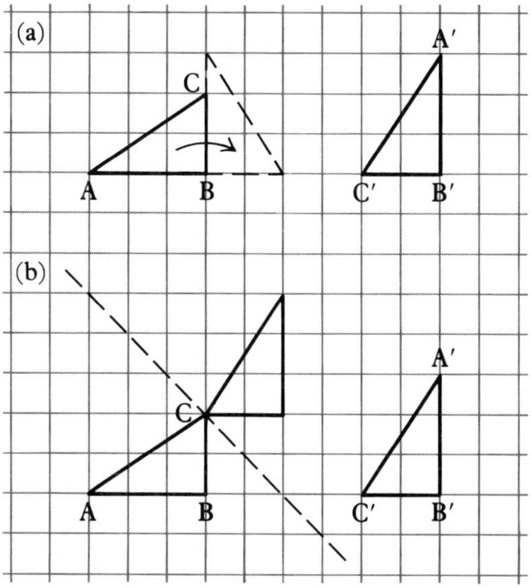

19.3 (a), (b)

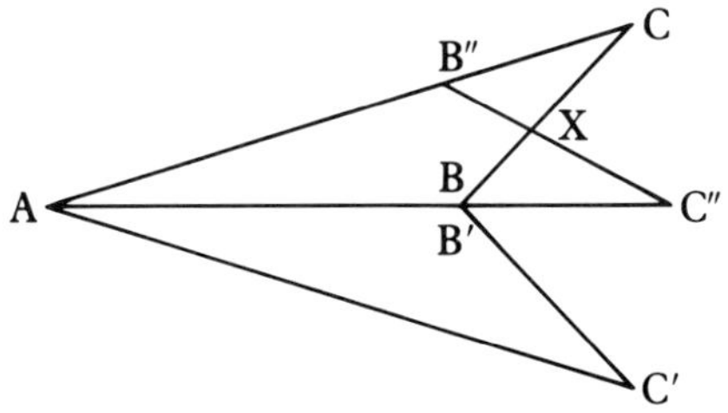

(c) Reflection in the line AX

20 Trigonometry

20.1 (a) 6·45 cm (b) 11·9 cm (c) 5·08 cm
(d) 8·30 cm (all to 3 s.f.)

20.2 (a) 30·1° (b) 35·5° (c) 70·3°
(d) 53·3° (all to 3 s.f.)

20.3 18·1 m (to 3 s.f.)

20.4 34·3° (to 3 s.f.)

20.5 (a) 21·0° (b) 9·61 m (both to 3 s.f.)

20.6 (a) 23·6° and 156·4°
(b) 143·1° and 216·9°

20.7 (a)

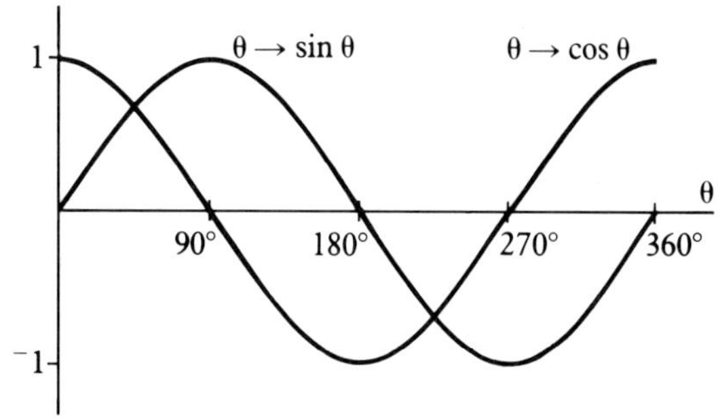

(b) 45° and 225°

21 Three dimensions

21.1

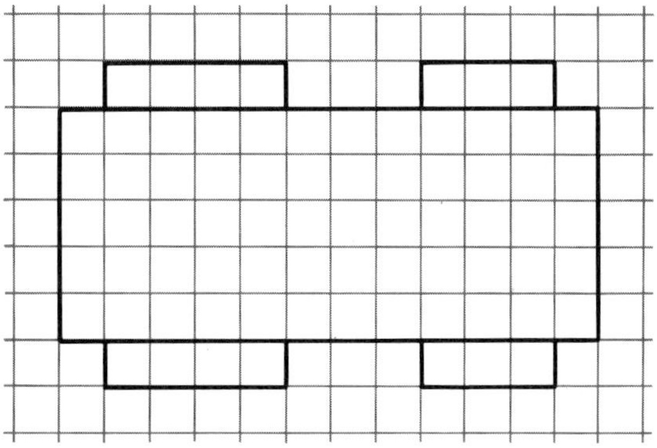

21.2 (a)

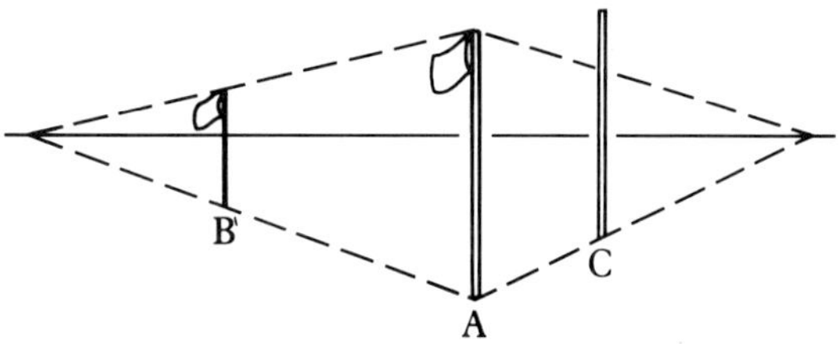

(b) C is about $\frac{1}{3}$ higher than A, so it is about 11 m tall.

21.3 (a)

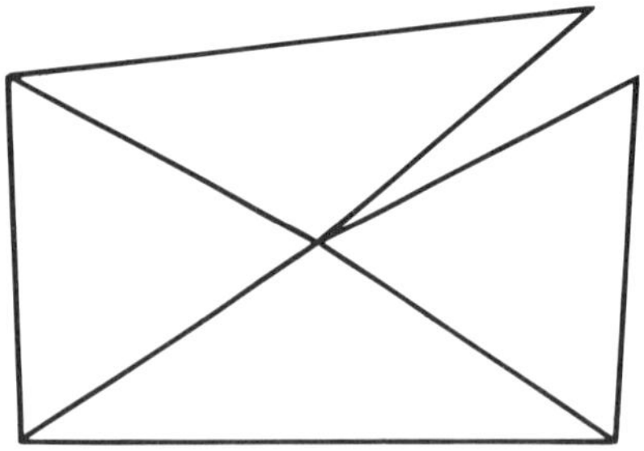

(b) About $16\,m^2$

(c) About 6 m (5·988 m by calculation)

21.4 (a) *a* 6 m, *b* 10 m, *c* 4 m, *d* 3 m, *e* 2 m, *f* 6 m

(b) Rectangular-based pyramid

(c) $78\,m^3$

21.5 (a) 3·61 m (b) 4·24 m (c) 4·69 m

(d) $89{\cdot}5\,m^2$ (e) 39·8° (all to 3 s.f.)

21.6 (a) $2360\,cm^2$ (b) 160 cm

(both to 3 s.f.)

21.7

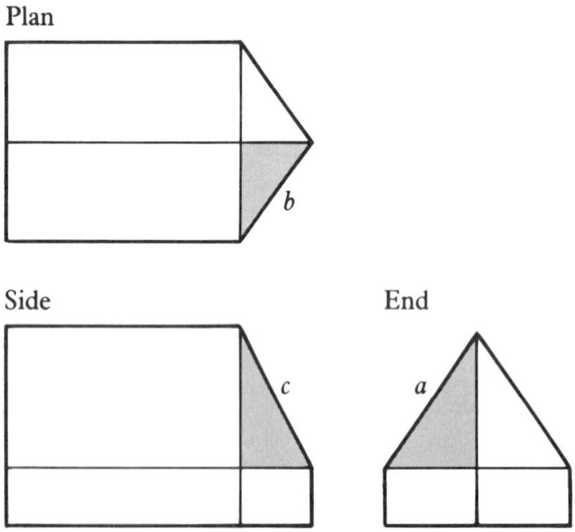

21.8 (a) (12, 0, 0)

(b) (12, 15, 0), (4, 0, 0), (4, 5, 0)

22 The Earth

22.1 (a) A 15°N 15°W, B 30°S 0°E/W, C 15°S 45°E, D 0°N/S 30°E, E 0°N/S 30°W, F 15°S 15°W

(b) 6670 km (c) 3340 km (both to 3 s.f.)

22.2 (a) 90° (b) 10 000 km

(c) 7660 km (to 3 s.f.)

(d) RS is too large in relation to PQ.

23 Enlargement and reduction

23.1 (a) 2·4 (b) 230·4 mm

(c) 182·4 mm by 18 mm

23.2 (a) 3276·8 kg (b) 9·6 litres

23.3 (a) $34{\cdot}2\,m^2$ (b) $136{\cdot}8\,cm^2$

24 Vector geometry

24.1 (a) $\underset{\sim}{a} + \underset{\sim}{b}$ (b) $\underset{\sim}{b} - \underset{\sim}{a}$ (c) $2\underset{\sim}{b} - 2\underset{\sim}{a}$

(d) $2\underset{\sim}{b} - \underset{\sim}{a}$ (e) $2\underset{\sim}{a} - \underset{\sim}{b}$

24.2 (a) (i) $2\underset{\sim}{b} - \underset{\sim}{a}$ (ii) $\underset{\sim}{b} - \frac{1}{2}\underset{\sim}{a}$ (iii) $\frac{1}{2}\underset{\sim}{a} + \underset{\sim}{b}$

(b) (i) $3\underset{\sim}{a} - 2\underset{\sim}{b}$ (ii) $\frac{3}{4}\underset{\sim}{a} - \frac{1}{2}\underset{\sim}{b}$ (iii) $\frac{3}{4}\underset{\sim}{a} + 1\frac{1}{2}\underset{\sim}{b}$

(c) $\overrightarrow{OF} = 1\frac{1}{2}\overrightarrow{OE}$

This means that O, E and F lie on a straight line.

25 Statistics

25.1 98·1 paper clips per box

25.2 (a) Species A 36 cm, species B 25·5 cm

(b) Species A 104 cm, species B 100·5 cm

(c) 66% (d) 53%

(e) Species A 12·5 cm, species B 7·5 cm (approx.)

(f) In species B, a higher proportion of lengths were close to the median value. The lengths of species A were more spread out.

(g)

Length in cm	Percentage of species A	Percentage of species B
80–85	2%	0%
85–90	7%	0%
90–95	10%	10%
95–100	15%	38%
100–105	21%	28%
105–110	20%	16%
110–115	16%	8%
115–120	9%	0%

Allow some variation.

(h)

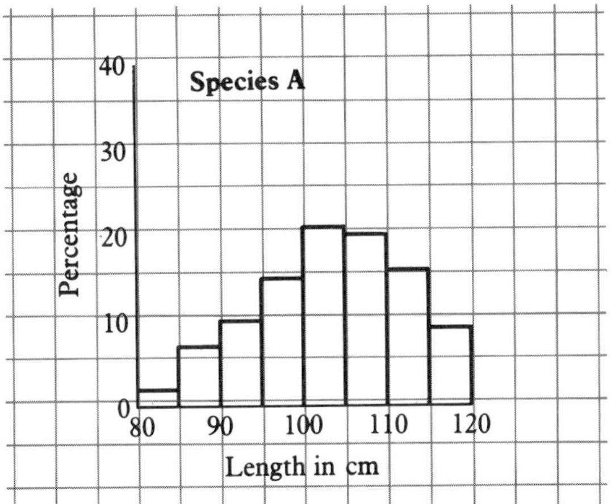

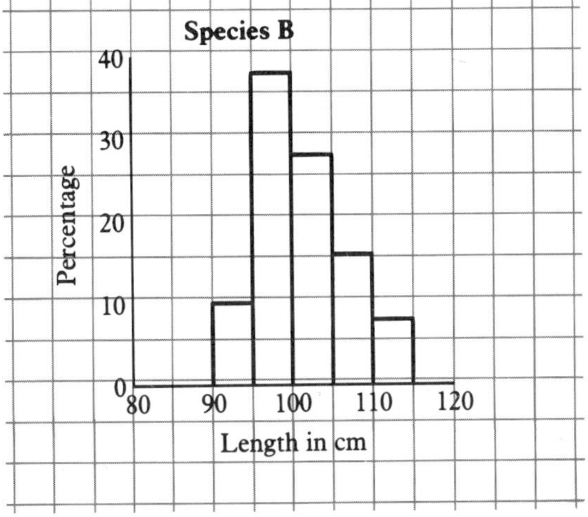

25.3 (a)

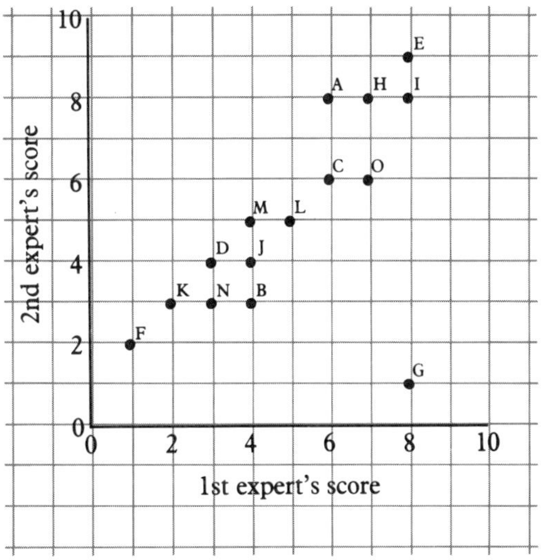

(b) Wine G (c) Yes
(d) They would lie on a line through the origin at 45° to the horizontal.
(e) 1st expert 5·2, 2nd expert 5·0
The 1st expert gave higher scores on average.
(f) You could take the mean score of each wine to get the following: E, I, H, A, O, C, L, G, M, J, B, D, N, K, F

26 Selections and arrangements

26.1 24 possible orders

26.2 (a) 28 possible combinations
(b) 39 combinations

26.3 It cannot be done with all eight. It can be done by leaving out D, E or H.
Without D, E or H is at one end, C or G at the other.
Without E, D or H is at one end, C or G at the other.
Without H, D or E is at one end, C or G at the other.

The associated network to solve the problem is

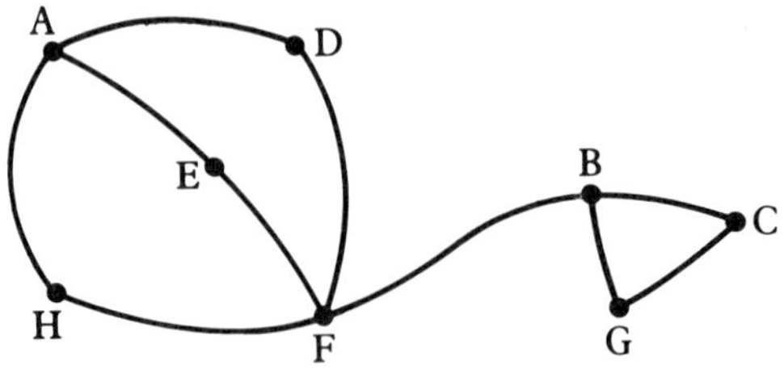

27 Probability

27.1 (a) 1,2 1,3 1,4 1,5
2,3 2,4 2,5
3,4 3,5
4,5

(b) $\frac{4}{10} = \frac{2}{5}$

27.2 $\frac{1}{1296} = 0{\cdot}000772$ (to 3 s.f.)

27·3 (a) $\frac{1}{20}$ (b) $\frac{7}{20}$ (c) $\frac{12}{20}$

27.4 (a)

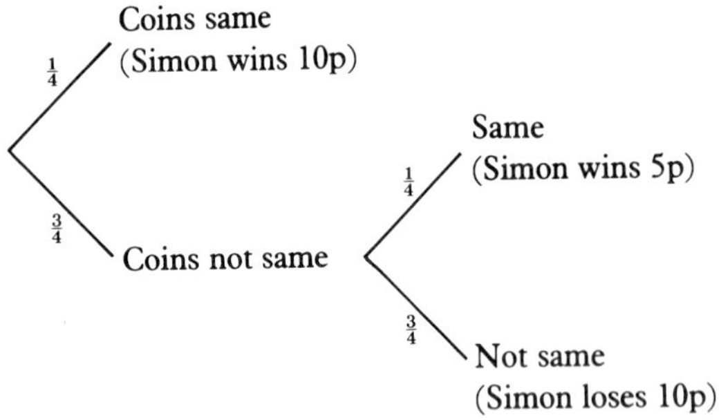

(b) (i) $\frac{1}{4}$ (ii) $\frac{3}{16}$ (iii) $\frac{9}{16}$

(c) You would expect him to lose about £22.

M Miscellaneous questions

M1 (a) 0·0423474 (b) 0·0423 (to 3 s.f.)

M2 $2{\cdot}998 \times 10^8$ m/s

M3 $x = 30$

M4 Generally, as the latitude gets higher, the temperature gets lower.

M5 (a) 0·5 (b) $y = 0{\cdot}5x - 1$

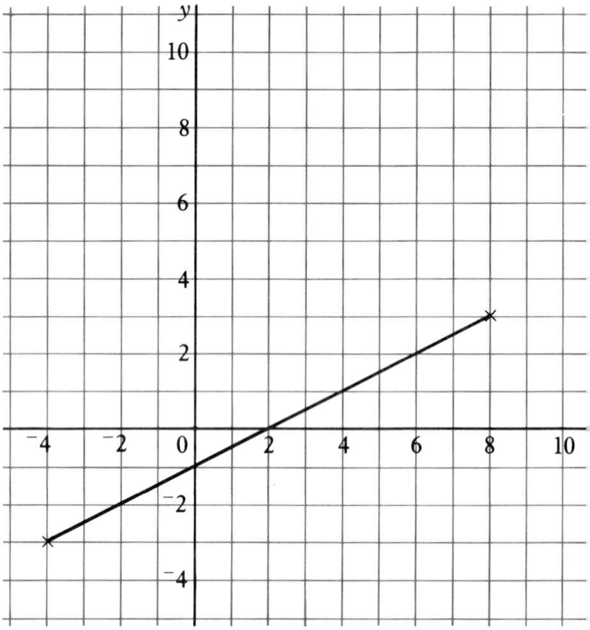

M6 (d) is the smallest.

M7 (a) (i) 393 cm (ii) 124 cm
(b) 78·6 m (c) 63·3 revolutions
(all to 3 s.f.)

M8 (a)

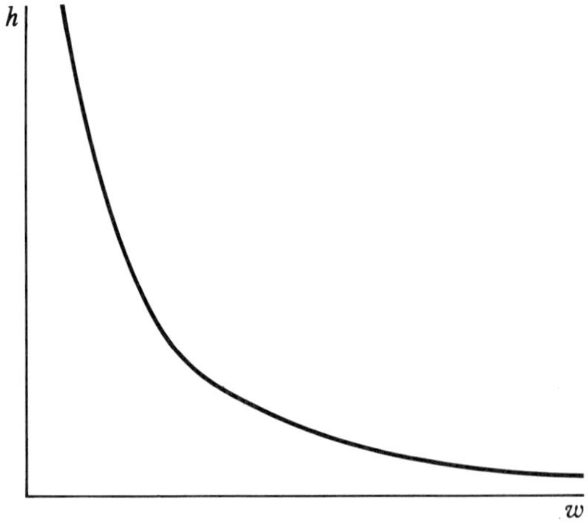

(b) h is doubled. (c) $h = 37{\cdot}5$

M9 (a) 8:16 a.m. (b) 8:30 a.m.

M10 (a) 360° (b) 540° (c) 100°

M11 (a) The frequency is doubled.
(b) (i) 1671 Hz (ii) 139·3 mm
(both to 4 s.f.)

M12 (a) (i) 278·7 m^2 (ii) 27 870 m^3
(b) (i) 18·29 m (ii) 33·68°
(all to 4 s.f.)

M13 (a) 31·0 m.p.h. (to 1 d.p.)
(b) (i)

d	50	100	150	200	250
$30d$	1500	3000	4500	6000	7500
$s = \sqrt{(30d)}$	38·7	54·8	67·1	77·5	86·6

(ii)

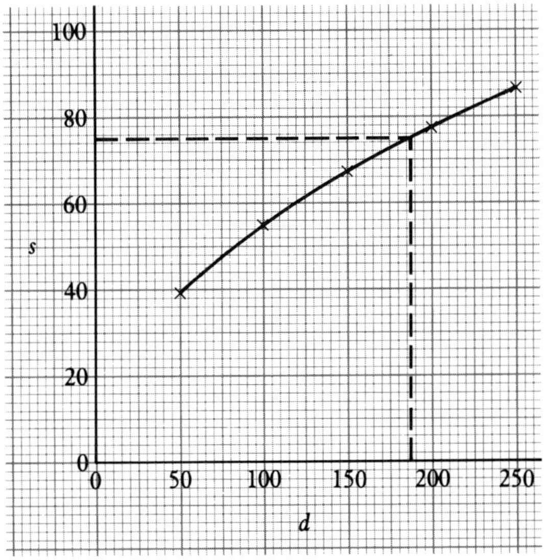

(iii) About 187 or 188 feet

M14 (a) (i) 3·6 microns (ii) 131·2 sq microns
(iii) 524·8 sq microns
(b) (i) 280·5 sq microns
(ii) 46·55% decrease (to 4 s.f.)

M15 (a) $1{\cdot}196\,91 \times 10^{-3}$ (b) 0·00119691

M16 (a) The next term is double the previous one. $u_{n+1} = 2u_n$
(b) $u_n = 3 \times 2^{n-1}$

M17 It will be multiplied by 9.

M18 D is about 50.

M19 $x = {}^{-}2$ or $x = 5$

M20 75 kg

M21 (a) (i) 75% (ii) 56·25%
(b) About 8 strokes

M22 About 28 000 matchboxes

M23 (a) Double and add 1.
(b) 127 (c) $s_{n+1} = 2s_n + 1$
(d) 2, 4, 8, 16, 32, 64
nth term $= 2^n$
(e) $s_n = 2^n - 1$

M24 (a) $y = p + qx$ (b) $x = y - \dfrac{p}{q}$

M25 (a) \$264·10
(b) £175·18 (to nearest penny)

M26 £121 737

M27 (a) 1, 0, $^{-}$0·25, $^{-}$0·3125, $^{-}$0·328 125
(b) $^{-}$0·333 333 (c) $^{-}\frac{1}{3}$

M28 0·2

M29 (a) (i) $x + y$ litres (ii) $20x + 80y$ grams
(b) 3·5 litres of weak and 2·5 litres of strong

M30 10 units

M31 (a), (b)

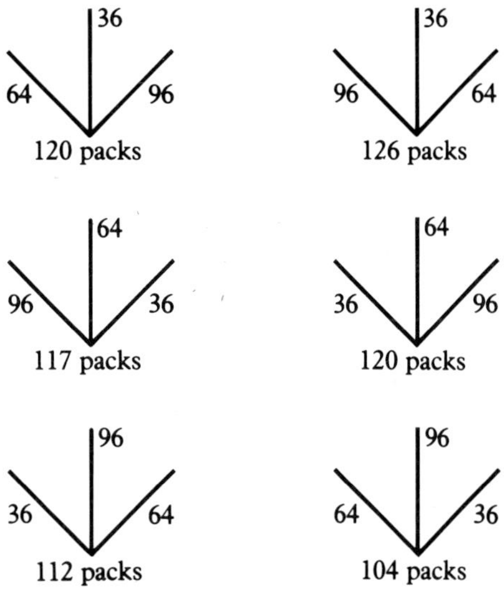

(c) (i) The maximum number of packs is 126. These could be packed in a box with internal dimensions of 288 mm × 216 mm × 448 mm.
(ii) Pupil's discussion of the various points of view the superstore may take

M32 (a) $\frac{1}{9}$ (b) $\frac{1}{81}$

M33 (a) 10 mm (b) 85·8 mm^2 (to 3 s.f.)
(c) 14·1 mm (to 3 s.f.)

M34 About 1·7 m

M35 (a) (i) 67·1 cm (ii) 73·4°
(b) (i)

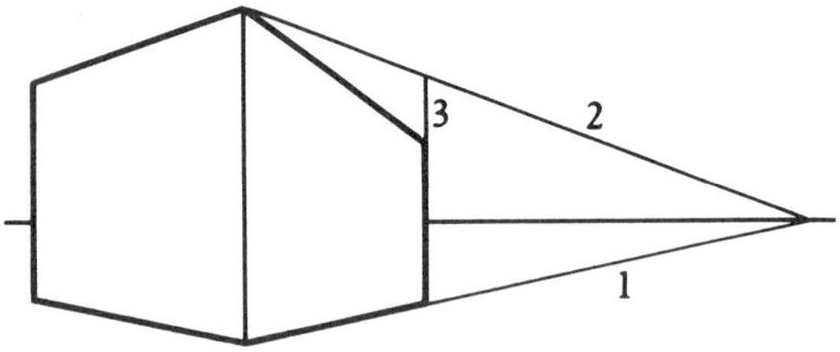

(ii) 147° (iii) 0·408 (iv) 334 cm
(all to 3 s.f.)

M36 (a) $(x + 2)(x - 3)$ (b) $x = -2$ or $x = 3$

M37 (a) 2400 m^2
(b) (i) Pupil's explanation
(ii) $x = 23{\cdot}0$

M38 (a) 6·9 cm^2 (b) 9 cm^2
(c) 10·4 cm^2 (d) 11·5 cm^2

Published by the Press Syndicate of the University of Cambridge
The Pitt Building, Trumpington Street, Cambridge CB2 1RP
40 West 20th Street, New York, NY 10011, USA
10 Stamford Road, Oakleigh, Melbourne 3166, Australia

First published 1987
Third printing 1990

Typesetting and diagrams by Marlborough Design
Printed in Great Britain at the University Press, Cambridge

ISBN 0 521 31474 7

ED